how to raise and train a
cairn terrier

by erliss mc cormack

The text of this book is the result of the joint efforts of the author and the editorial staff of T.F.H. Publications, Inc., which is the originator of all sections of the book except the chapter dealing with the history and standard of the breed. Additionally, the portrayal of canine pet products in this book is for general instructive value only; their appearance does not necessarily constitute an endorsement by either the author or publisher.

Distributed in the UNITED STATES by T.F.H. Publications, Inc., 211 West Sylvania Avenue, Neptune City, NJ 07753; in CANADA by Rolf C. Hagen Ltd., 3225 Sartelon Street, Montreal 382 Quebec; in ENGLAND by T.F.H. (Great Britain) Ltd., 11 Ormside Way, Holmethorpe Industrial Estate, Redhill, Surrey RH1 2PX; in AUSTRALIA AND THE SOUTH PACIFIC by Pet Imports Pty. Ltd., Box 149 Brookvale 2100 N.S.W., Australia; in SOUTH AFRICA by Multipet (Pty.) Ltd., 30 Turners Avenue, Durban 4001. Published by T.F.H. Publications Inc. Ltd., The British Crown Colony of Hong Kong.

Contents

The ideal Cairn Terrier should have a harsh coat which must not be curly. However, a slightly wavy coat is acceptable.

1. History, Description, and Standard

HISTORY OF THE BREED

The Cairn Terrier originated over two hundred years ago in the Highlands of Scotland and on the Isle of Skye. The early history of the Cairn is so vague that so far as can be determined, no one has been able to discover the breed's exact origin. It is an indisputable fact that the Cairn is one of the oldest, if not the oldest, pure British terrier breed, and its place of origin is immaterial. Records go back to the 16th century, when historians wrote of the "earth dogs" from Argyllshire. Turberville and Dr. Caius, in their writings, refer to the "terriers of the North" as early as the Elizabethan days; John Leslie, another writer, a century earlier makes note of a small breed of terrier used for hunting foxes and badgers in Scotland. There is no conclusive proof, but it is believed that these dogs must have been ancestors of the present day Cairn and that the modern day Scottish Terriers also have evolved from this same ancestor.

It is also known that King James VI of Scotland gave, as a present, a half dozen of the "earth dogs" to a friend in France. He instructed that they be obtained from Argyllshire and that they be sent in at least two ships.

Because these early terriers were used in hunting foxes, badgers, and other small fur-bearing vermin which were to be found in the rocky crevices, or cairns, they were named Cairn Terriers. The name Terrier comes from the Latin "terra" meaning the earth. It was the Cairn's job to go into these dens or cairns after the vermin and to worry his game until it would come out, to be killed by the dog's master.

It is believed that the oldest known strain of Cairns was founded by the late Capt. MacLeod of Drynoch, Isle of Skye. Records have been found in several old Scottish families pertaining to dogs owned by earlier members. The best known are those of the MacDonalds of Waternish and the Drynoch strains of the MacLeods, both of which came from the Isle of Skye. In the MacDonald kennel, the darker grays or brindles seemed to be prominent while the silver grays dominated the Drynoch strain. Another early kennel was the Mackinnon of Kilbride where color variation was from cream to nearly black.

Other early pioneers of the breed were Mrs. Alastair Campbell and The Hon. Mary Hawke. It was through the perseverance of these two ladies that the Cairn Terrier was finally recognized by the Kennel Club in 1910. Previous to this, Cairns were known as prick-eared Skye terriers or short-haired Skye Terriers and shown under this classification.

EARLY SHOW HISTORY

The first recognizable entry of a Cairn Terrier appeared in the June 1907 issue of the Kennel Gazette as follows: "Calla-mhor, b Mrs. I. A. Campbell by Mr. N. Nicholson's Fearg-Speraig, April 1894." In the same issue the notification of the registration of Cuillean Bhan appeared, also in the name of Mrs. Campbell, out of the same bitch, but sired by Mr. Harris' Brassy and born in March, 1905. The only other registration in 1907 was that of Roy Mhor, which appeared in the November issue in the name of Mrs. Campbell where she was given as the owner of both the sire and the dam, Morghan and Calla-mhor respectively. In 1908 there were only two registrations, both in the name of Mrs. Alastair Campbell. In fact, the first seven Cairns (registered as Prick-Eared Skye Terriers) were registered in her name. Later she became the first Secretary of the Cairn Terrier Club and she judged the first show at which championship status was granted the breed. She bred "Firring Flora" who was the first bitch to win a challenge certificate. She owned the first dog champion, "Ch. Gesto."

In 1909, the number registered had increased to 14 and in 1910, 35 were registered. It was during this year also that the Cairn Terriers already registered as Skye Terriers were transferred to the new registry.

In 1924, The Kennel Club (British) ceased to accept for registration the progeny of Cairn Terrier and West Highland crosses. Prior to this, white puppies of such matings had been accepted as West Highland White Terriers, while the darker pups of the same litters were registered as Cairn Terriers. This action followed the precedent set by the American Kennel Club.

It is interesting to note that some of the earlier breeders carry the names of Twobees, O'the Braes, Thistleclose, Redletter, and Rhu. These same names are found in the pedigrees of many present-day winners.

Cairn Terriers were first registered in the United States in 1913. In 1950 they were in 42nd place among all breeds and in 1963 registrations had jumped to place the breed in 36th place, an increase of 2.4 per cent, and from 532 registrations to 1,270 or more than double. Their pleasing personality, their friendliness, their ability to learn, and the constant desire to please, has steadily increased the popularity of the Cairn as a family pet and companion and has brought about this increase.

In England, of the 100 or more breeds registered today, the Cairn is 11th in popularity and is the most popular terrier.

DESCRIPTION

The Cairn is a little dog that loves people. Dogs that have been kenneled for years adapt very readily and make perfect house pets. Even the wildest become very gentle in the home and there is no need to think that being "in" will spoil them; they love people and hate being away from them.

In early days the Cairn was often used for hunting otter. No terrier could match him at this. Today the Cairn is an

An outdoor dog show scene in England. Cairns are quite popular in Great Britain and are to be seen in many of the large dog shows there.

To prepare a Cairn Terrier for a show, the dog should be bathed, groomed and trimmed being careful to not destroy his "rough and shaggy" look.

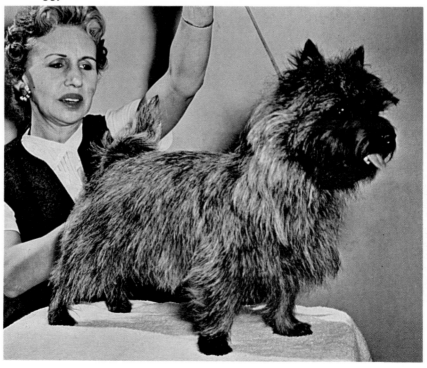

In temperament, Cairns are gregarious dogs and live compatibly with one another. The early Cairns were pack dogs kept by Scottish Lairds to control the predatory animals, like foxes, badgers and others, found in the rocky areas near their farms.

equally good hunter and nothing pleases him more than the fresh scent of a small varmint, rat, gopher, or other burrowing animal. He is a born digger and if there is a juicy scent of some little pest in the middle of milady's rose bed, he will often dig after and come up with the offender. Farmers who have several Cairns are seldom troubled with mice, rats, or other rodents in their hay and grain.

The Cairn is double-coated. He has a good, thick, wooly undercoat and a long, harsh outercoat, to resist the weather. The Cairn should carry his tail high at a perpendicular angle and never hooked over his back. The word "shaggy" in describing the Cairn fits him very well; however, he should not be described as untidy or unkempt. The ideal size of the Cairn Terrier should be 14 lbs. for dogs, 13 lbs. for bitches.

The Cairn Terrier may be any color, except pure white. The most common colors are wheaten gray, red, or the same colors with brindle shadings and mostly with black points (black tipped around the ears and black masks). A listing of Cairn colors published in 1936 included twenty-four shades or mixture of colors.

The Cairn color is very hard to determine in a puppy. I have seen a beautiful silver gray at two months become golden or even a brindle at 5 or 6 months. Puppy fluff can be very misleading; it usually looks silvery or tan, with darker ends. Generally, the color can usually be determined by the shade of the coat coming in around the eyes.

There is no rule regarding breeding for color as is the case in some breeds. I have known of a red bitch bred to a silver male and the result was two white puppies. This is not so odd as it may seem. The lines of Harbestoun and Moccassin both run back to Athol, who was white, coming down from Morfen and Snowdrift—also white, and who might also be found in some Westie pedigrees. White Cairns, as stated before, are no longer acceptable, but a cream, with dark points at birth, will often look lighter with age and lose those dark points. Tan puppies with black points will turn up in some lines—these usually turn gray by the time they are about a year old. I once heard of a litter that had 3 puppies with white collars at birth. By the time the puppies were approximately 3 months of age, they had not only changed their color completely—but not a white hair was left, and all three of the puppies were very dark.

PERSONALITY

The Cairn Terrier is a small dog, light-footed and sturdy, with a true "foxy" look about him. The Cairn expression is like nothing else in the world. The eyes should be small, dark and piercing, fox-like in expression—a mixture of gentleness, cunningness and fierceness. The Cairn is cunning to the point that he resembles a fox in many ways. Cairns are gentle and loving and have an intense desire to please their masters. They are intelligent, full of spirit, but not high-strung. They are protective of home and family to a point that seems almost unbelievable for such a small dog. They will sound an alarm, catch rodents and similar pests, stand between you and an angry bull. They are not fighters—they will not deliberately pick a fight as will other terrier breeds—yet they will stand their ground and in no sense of the word can be called cowardly. They are not barkers, but will warn of a prowler or other out of the ordinary circumstances. These qualities make the Cairn Terrier an excellent all-around companion and family pet. It has often been said that if you have a Cairn Terrier in your home for a year, you will have one the rest of your life.

You won't find a Cairn having the colors and furnishings of some other breeds, but rather the beauty of this little dog comes from his heart. He has the desire to please and seeks to do for others, not for himself. He can be a house dog or an outdoor dog. He is easily adaptable and most versatile. Cairns are kept by people in all walks of life. They are at home in a small apartment, a large mansion—in the city or

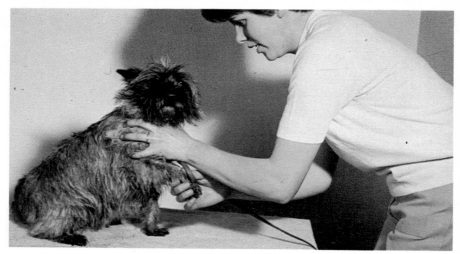

"Shaking hands" is one of the simple tricks your young Cairn can learn quickly.

A natural born digger and chaser, a Cairn Terrier will "fetch" or retrieve a moving object on command.

The "foxy" expression of a Cairn Terrier is enhanced by trimming off the long hairs of the ears.

on a farm. They are boys' dogs! They like nothing better than a good romp. They love the water and are typical outdoor dogs, always ready for a swim, a fishing trip or a hike in the woods. On the other hand, they are equally suited to little girls, and their quiet temperament comes forth. This friendly little dog can always find his place and capture the hearts of his owners and all who know him.

STANDARD FOR THE CAIRN TERRIER

GENERAL APPEARANCE: Active, game, small, working terrier of the short-legged type; very free in his movements, strongly but not heavily built. He stands well forward on his forelegs, is deep in the ribs, well coupled with strong hindquarters and presenting a well-proportioned body with a medium-length back, having a hard, weather-resistant coat. The head is shortest and widest among all other terriers and well furnished with hair giving a general foxy expression.

HEAD: Skull broad in proportion to length with a definite stop; top of head well furnished with hair that may be somewhat softer than the body coat. Muzzle is strong but not too long or heavy, with mouth neither overshot nor undershot and with large teeth. Nose is black and eyes are set wide apart, rather sunken, with shaggy eyebrows, of medium size, hazel or dark hazel in color depending on body color. Ears are small, pointed, carried erect, set wide apart on the side of the head and free from long hairs.

BODY: Well-muscled, strong, with well-sprung, deep ribs, coupled to strong hindquarters, and with a level back of medium length. Shoulders are sloping.

LEGS AND FEET: Forelegs must be perfectly straight, should not be out at the elbows, although the forefeet may be slightly turned. Forefeet are larger than hind feet. Legs must be covered with hard hair. Pads should be thick and strong and dog must stand well on his feet.

TAIL: In proportion to head, well furnished with hair but not feathery, carried gaily but not curled over back and is set on back level.

COAT AND COLOR: Coat is hard and weather-resistant; must be double-coated, the outer coat harsh and profuse, the undercoat close, soft and furry. Any color except white is permissible and dark ears, muzzle and tail tip are desirable.

IDEAL SIZE: Weight for bitches, 13 pounds; for dogs, 14 pounds. Height at the withers for bitches, 9½ inches; for dogs, 10 inches. Body length, measured from the front of the chest to back of hindquarters, should be 14¼ to 15 inches. Dog must be of balanced proportions, neither leggy nor too low, and neither too long nor too short in body length. These weights and measurements apply to mature dogs (2 years old). Older dogs may weigh slightly more and growing dogs may be under these weights and measurements.

CONDITION: A dog when shown should be in good hard flesh, well-muscled, neither too fat nor too thin. He should have a full good coat with plenty of head furnishings, be clean, combed, brushed and tidied up completely. On a loose leash his movement is free and easy.

FAULTS: *Skull:* Too narrow. *Muzzle:* Foreface too long and heavy, mouth overshot or undershot. *Eyes:* Too large, prominent, yellow and ringed eyes are all objectionable. *Ears:* Too large, round at points, set too close together, set too high on head, heavily covered with hair. *Legs and Feet:* Too light or too heavy bone, crooked forelegs or out at elbow, too high or too low on the leg. Thin, ferrety feet. Feet let down on heel, or too open or spread. *Body:* Too short back and compact body. Body too long, weedy and snaky. Tail set too low. Back not level. *Coat:* Open coats, blousy coats, too short or dead coats, lack of sufficient undercoat, lack of hard hair on legs. Silkiness or curliness (a slight wave permissible). *Nose:* Flesh or light-colored. *Color:* White on chest, feet or other parts of body.

Since they originated from the same ancestral dog, the striking similarity between a Cairn Terrier and a West Highland Terrier is very evident. To preserve the integrity of these two breeds, the offspring of Cairn and West Highland crossings cannot be registered in the United States or other countries.

GROOMING THE CAIRN TERRIER

The importance of grooming cannot be overemphasized. Next to proper feeding, grooming is next in importance. Proper grooming is essential to the Cairn's well-being and comfort. A clean, well-groomed dog is a healthy, happy dog. By keeping the coat brushed and clean, numerous skin troubles can be avoided. Dead hair should be brushed out and this will help reduce shedding.

If hair becomes matted, a good bath and the assistance of a tool called a *mat and tangle splitter* will help to relieve the situation. There are also several grooming preparations on the market today that will help to remove mats when used before bathing. The necessary grooming equipment should consist of a brush (slicker type with metal teeth set in rubber), claw clippers, a pair of thinning scissors, a pair of good barber scissors, a comb (I like the double kind with both coarse and fine teeth) and a good bristle brush.

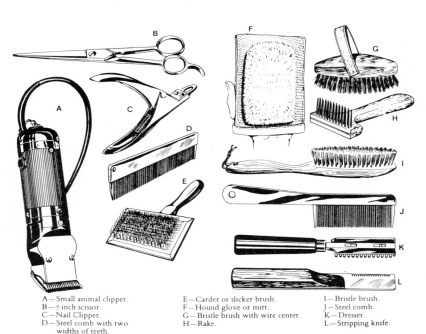

A—Small animal clipper.
B—7 inch scissor.
C—Nail Clipper.
D—Steel comb with two widths of teeth.

E—Carder or slicker brush.
F—Hound glove or mitt.
G—Bristle brush with wire center.
H—Rake.

I—Bristle brush.
J—Steel comb.
K—Dresser.
L—Stripping knife.

Daily grooming need not be given, but the Cairn owner should establish a grooming routine of at least two or three times each week. Brushing the coat stimulates the oil glands and as a result the dog's coat will look more sleek and shiny and he will do less scratching. A well-cared-for dog is a pleasure to have around and the dog soon learns to enjoy this routine and seems all the more proud of his own neat appearance. Whenever you do work on your dog, remember that short sessions are better than long ones. Do not work so long that your dog becomes overtired and unruly.

During the grooming, the dog should be checked for fleas, lice, ticks, etc. Keep in mind that a scratching dog cannot have a good coat and there must be a cause for this condition. Many good dog shampoos on the market today contain a formula to rid the dog of these pests. A shampoo should be used that contains an oil base and will not rob the dog of his natural oils. The coat should be brushed while drying. A regular hair dryer can be used to dry the dog. The coat should not be brushed when it is dry. There are many commercial preparations in spray containers that may be used as grooming aids.

The leg furnishings and whiskers should be handled with a great deal of care as it takes a long time for them to grow and rough handling can result in their breaking off. The coat around the feet should be trimmed. The excess hair underneath and between the toes should be trimmed out and the feet tidied.

The Cairn Terrier does not need to be stripped as is the case of the hard-coated Terriers. However, when a puppy is about 3 to 4 months of age, it is a good idea to remove the puppy coat with the aid of a stripping knife or other plucking tool. A denser more beautiful coat will grow in as a result. This is usually done again at approximately one year of age, or when the coat is becoming loosened and is ready to fall out.

Regular brushing not only removes dirt, grime, loose hairs and dead skin, but it also stimulates circulation of blood to the skin and secretion of oil by the glands of the skin.

A good strong comb (preferably of metal, such as steel) is recommended for removing snarls. However, the comb should not be pulled through the hair without first supporting the strands close to the skin.

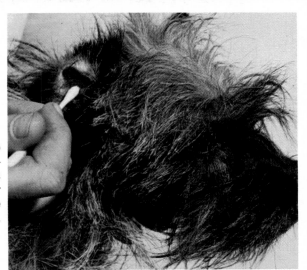

A cotton-tipped swab is just right for cleaning the ears. Always inspect the ears after bathing, to remove any droplets of water.

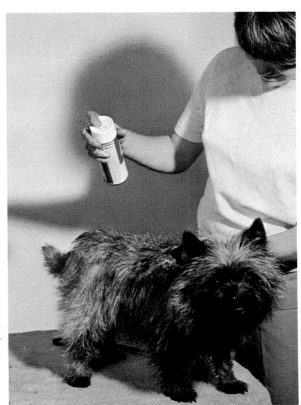

Spray your dog in an area with good air circulation only. Most insecticides contain strong chemicals and breathing in such substances can be harmful both to your dog and yourself.

2. Buying Your Cairn Terrier

Now that you have decided on this breed, it is time to go about getting him—or her.

You'll have to make up your mind about whether you want a male or a female, an adult or a puppy, a show dog or "just a pet". There is no greater use for a dog than being 'just' a beloved pet and companion, but the dog which has profitable show and breeding possibilities is worth more to the seller.

PET OR SHOW DOG

The puppy with a slight flaw in his ear carriage or quantity of coat will make just as good a companion and guardian, but his more perfect litter mate will cost more.

That is why there is often a difference in price between puppies which look—to you, anyway—identical. If you think you may eventually want to show your dog or raise a litter of puppies, by all means buy the best you can afford. You will save expense and disappointment later on. However, if the puppy is *strictly* a pet for the children, or companion for you, you can afford to look for a bargain. The pup which is not show material; the older pup, for which there is often less demand; or the grown dog, not up to being used for breeding, are occasionally available and are opportunities to save money. Remember that these are the only real bargains in buying a dog. It takes good food and care—and plenty of both—to raise a puppy.

The price you pay for your dog is little compared to the love and devotion he will return over the many years he'll be with you. With good care and affection, your pup should live to a ripe old age; through modern veterinary science and nutrition, dogs are better cared for and living longer. The average life expectancy is twelve years, and dogs in their teens are not uncommon.

MALE OR FEMALE CAIRN

If you should intend breeding your dog in the future, by all means buy a female. You can find a suitable mate without difficulty when the time comes, and have the pleasure of raising a litter of pups—there is nothing cuter than a fat, playful puppy. If you don't want to raise puppies, your female can be spayed, and will remain a healthy, lively pet. The female is smaller than the male and generally quieter. She has less tendency to roam in search of romance, but a properly trained male can be a charming pet, and has a certain difference in temperament that is appealing to many people. Male vs. female is chiefly a matter of personal choice.

ADULT OR PUP

Whether to buy a grown dog or a small puppy is another question. It is undeniably fun to watch your dog grow all the way from a baby, sprawling and playful, to a mature, dignified dog. If you don't have the time to spend on the more frequent meals, housebreaking, and other training a puppy needs in order to become a dog you can be proud of, then choose an older, partly trained pup or a grown dog. If you want a show dog, remember that no one, not even an expert, can predict with 100 percent accuracy what a small puppy will be like when he grows up. He may be right *most* of the time, but six months is the earliest age for the would-be exhibitor to pick a prospect and know that his future is relatively safe.

If you have a small child, it is best to get a puppy big enough to defend himself, one not less than four or five months old. Older children will enjoy playing with and helping to take care of a baby pup, but at less than four months, a puppy wants to do little but eat and sleep, and he must be protected from teasing and overtiring. You cannot expect a very young child to understand that a puppy is a fragile living being.

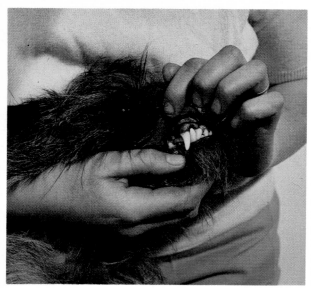

Any slight disorder in the mouth should be attended to with little delay. Loose teeth, sore gums, broken teeth can result in dental decay and subsequent loss of teeth.

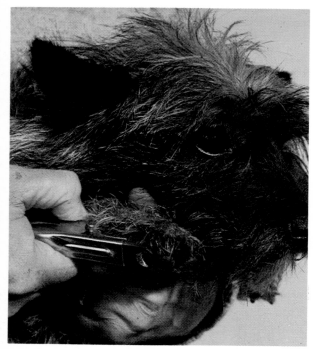

Do not attempt to trim the toenails when your pet is agitated to avoid the possibility of cutting into the quick. Take your time, be extra careful and cut a little at a time.

Occasionally, it will be necessary to give your dog a bath. To minimize his fear, never use very cold water or allow soap or shampoo to get into his eyes, ears and nose.

After a thorough rinsing and most of the water has drained off, take him out of the tub, and dry him off before he shakes and possibly sprays you with water.

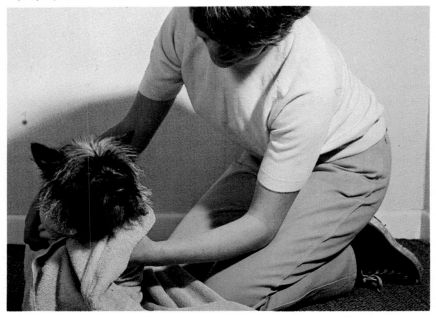

WHERE TO BUY A CAIRN TERRIER

You can choose among several places to buy your dog. One is a kennel which breeds show dogs as a business and has extra pups for sale as pets. Another is the one-dog owner who wants to sell the puppies from an occasional litter, paying for the expenses being his chief aim. Pet shops usually buy puppies from overstocked kennels or part-time hobbyists for re-sale, and you can generally buy a puppy there at a reasonable price. To find any of these, watch the pet column of your local newspaper or look in the classified section of your phone book. If you or your friends go driving out in the countryside, be on the lookout for a sign announcing pure-bred puppies for sale.

Whichever source you try, you can usually tell in a very short time whether the puppies will make healthy and happy pets. If they are clean, fat and lively, they are probably in good health. At the breeder's, you will have the advantage of seeing the puppies' mother and perhaps the father and other relatives. Remember that the mother, having just raised a demanding family, won't be looking her best, but if she is sturdy, friendly and well-mannered, her puppies should be too. If you feel that something is lacking in the care or condition of the dogs, it is better to look elsewhere than to buy hastily and regret it afterward.

You may be impatient to bring home your new dog, but a few days will make little difference in his life with you. Often it is a good idea to choose a puppy and put a deposit on him, but wait to take him home until you have prepared for the new arrival.

If you cannot find the dog you want locally, write to the secretary of the national breed club or kennel club and ask for names of breeders near you, or to whom you can write for information. Puppies are often bought by mail from reputable breeders. Pictures and pedigree information can be sent by breeders, who also can supply you with further details and helpful guidance.

Where you buy your puppy depends on what you want, just as the type of dog you choose depends on you.

WHAT TO LOOK FOR IN A CAIRN PUPPY

In choosing your puppy, assuming that it comes from healthy, wellbred parents, look for one that is friendly and out-going. The biggest pup in the litter is apt to be somewhat coarse as a grown dog, while the appealing "poor little runt" may turn out to be a timid shadow—or have a Napoleon complex! If you want a show dog and have no experience in choosing the prospect, study the standard, but be advised by the breeder on the finer points of conformation.

Now that you have paid your money and made your choice, you are ready to depart with puppy, papers and instructions. Make sure that you know his feeding routine, and take along some of the food. It is best to make any diet changes gradually so as not to upset his digestion. If the puppy is not fed before leaving he will ride comfortably on your lap where he can see out of the window. Take along a rag or newspapers for accidents.

PEDIGREES

When you buy your puppy you should receive his pedigree and registration certificate or application. These have nothing to do with licensing, which is a local regulation applying to pure-bred and mongrel alike. Find out the local ordinance in regard to age, etc., buy a license, and keep it on your dog whenever he is off your property.

Your dog's pedigree is a chart, for your information only, showing his ancestry. It is not part of his official papers. The registration certificate is the important part. If the dog was named and registered by his breeders you will want to complete the transfer and send it, with the proper fee, to the national kennel club. In the United States, this would

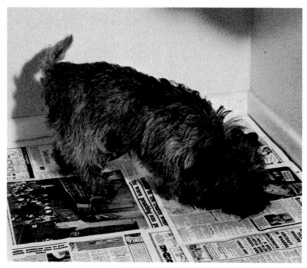

(Left) It is best not to change the location of the relief area preferred by your pet. He is guided to the same spot by his strong sense of smell.

(Below) If you do not want your pet to sleep on your couch or bed, give him a warm, comfortable place of his own.

A choke chain is safe, easy to use and inexpensive.

(Below) For total control of your dog's actions, he must learn to "heel" or to walk along beside you, on your left side, on or off the leash.

be the American Kennel Club (51 Madison Avenue, New York, NY 10010). They will transfer the dog to your ownership in their records, and send a new certificate to you.

If you receive instead an application for registration, you should fill it out, choosing a name for your pup, and mail it with the proper fee to the club. Be sure that the number of the puppy's litter is included.

3. Care of the Cairn Terrier Puppy

BRINGING YOUR CAIRN TERRIER HOME

When you bring your puppy home, remember that he is used to the peace and relative calm of a life of sleeping, eating and playing with his brothers and sisters. The trip away from all this is an adventure in itself, and so is adapting to a new home. So let him take it easy for a while. Don't let the whole neighborhood pat and poke him at one time. Be particularly careful when children want to handle him, for they cannot understand the difference between a delicate living puppy and the toy dog they play with and maul. If the puppy is to grow up loving children and taking care of them, he must not get a bad first impression.

FEEDING YOUR CAIRN TERRIER PUPPY

It is best to use the feeding schedule to which the puppy is accustomed, and stick to it except when you feel you can modify or improve it. You will probably want to feed the puppy on one of the commercially prepared dog foods as a base, flavoring it with table scraps and probably a little meat and fat when you have them. Remember that the dog food companies have prepared their food so that it is a balanced ration in itself, and, indeed, many dogs are raised on dog food alone. If you try to change this balance too much you are likely to upset your pet's digestion, and the dog will not be as well fed in the long run. Either kibble or meal is a good basic food, and the most economical way to feed your dog.

Milk is good for puppies and some grown dogs like it. Big bones are fine to chew on, especially for teething puppies, but small bones such as chicken, chop or fish bones are always dangerous; they may splinter or stick in the digestive tract. Table scraps such as meat, fat, or vegetables will furnish variety and vitamins, but fried or starchy foods such as potatoes and beans will not be of much food value. Adding a tablespoon of fat (lard or drippings) to the daily food will keep your puppy's skin healthy and make his coat shine.

Remember that all dogs are individuals. It is the amount that will keep your dog in good health which is right for him, not the "rule-book" amount. A feeding chart to give you some idea of what the average puppy will eat follows:

WEANING TO 3 MONTHS: *A.M.* dog food, mixed with warm water. *Noon* milk; cereal, kibble, or biscuits. *P.M.* dog food; meat; fat, scraps. *Bedtime* milk; biscuit.

3—6 MONTHS: *A.M.* dog meal or kibble, mixed. *Noon* milk; soft-boiled egg twice a week. *P.M.* meal, as above.

6 MONTHS—1 YEAR: *A.M.* dog meal, or milk with kibble. *P.M.* meal with meat, fat, scraps.

OVER 1 YEAR: *A.M.* half of evening meal if you prefer. *P.M.* meal, as above.

You may wish to try (although we do not necessarily recommend) a system of self-feeding instead of giving your puppy regular meals. This means keeping dry meal or kibble in front of him all the time. If he is inclined to overeat, do not put out more than he can easily consume each day.

Feed your dog at regular times and at the same place. A slight reprimand is in order if he scatters his food when eating.

A small reward in the form of an appetizing tidbit can perk up your pet during the tedium of training.

THE PUPPY'S BED

It is up to you to decide where the puppy will sleep. Unless it is winter in a cold climate, even a young puppy can sleep outside in a snug, well-built dog house. It should have a tight, pitched roof to let the rain run off and a floor off the ground, to avoid dampness. The door should be no larger than the grown dog will need to go in and out, as a bigger opening lets in too much draft. For bedding you can use an old rag or blanket, straw, or sweet-smelling cedar shavings. Whether the puppy sleeps indoors or out, he will benefit from an outdoor run of his own where he can be put to exercise and amuse himself. It does not have to be large, for if he goes for walks and plays with you he will get enough exercise that way. He is much safer shut in his run than being left loose to follow a stray dog off your property and get into bad habits—if he isn't hit by a car first!

Of course if the dog is left in his run for any length of time he should have protection from the cold, rain or sun. The run should be rectangular, and as big as you can conveniently make it up to 20 feet x 40 feet, with strong wire fence which will keep your dog in and intruders out. The wire should be high enough to prevent jumping, as many dogs like to jump, and the gate should be fastened with a spring hook or hasp that is not likely to become unfastened by chance.

If your dog sleeps indoors, he should have his own place and not be allowed to climb all over the furniture. He should sleep out of drafts, but not right next to the heat, which would make him too sensitive to the cold when he goes outside. If your youngster wants him to sleep on his bed, that is all right too, but the puppy must learn the difference between his bed and other furniture. He may sleep on a dog bed or in a box big enough to curl up in: a regulation dog crate or one made from a packing box, with bedding for comfort. If your cellar is dry and fairly warm the puppy will be all right there, or in the garage.

Vitamins and minerals are very much a part of the balanced diet of a dog. Supplements come in various forms, such as tablets, powder, and liquid, and a large assortment can be found in your local pet shop. The general condition of a dog is dependent on a proper balance of certain nutrients.

Both kibbled and canned dog food provide nourishment in a palatable way. Biscuits, in addition to containing good ingredients, also provide exercise for the teeth and gums. Such dog food is readily available, convenient to store, and easy to prepare.

Pet shops stock a variety of dog beds in different price ranges. Here is a unique example of one from Crown Products.

You have already decided where the puppy will sleep before you bring him home. Let him stay there, or in the corner he will soon learn is "his," most of the time, so that he will gain a sense of security from the familiar. Give the puppy a little milk with bread or kibble in it when he arrives, but don't worry if he isn't hungry at first. He will soon develop an appetite when he grows accustomed to his surroundings. The first night the puppy may cry a bit from lonesomeness, but if he has an old blanket or rug to curl up in he will be cozy. In winter a hot water bottle will help replace the warmth of his littermates, or the ticking of a clock may provide company.

HOUSEBREAKING YOUR PUPPY

As soon as you get your puppy you can begin to housebreak him but remember that you can't expect too much of him until he is five months old or so. A baby puppy just cannot control himself, so it is best to give him an opportunity to relieve himself before the need arises.

Don't let the puppy wander through the whole house; keep him in one or two rooms under your watchful eye. If he sleeps in the house and has been brought up on newspapers, keep a couple of pages handy on the floor. When he starts to whimper, puts his nose to the ground or runs around looking restless, take him to the paper before an "accident" occurs. After he has behaved, praise him and let him roam again. It is much better to teach him the right way than to punish him for misbehaving. Puppies are naturally clean and can be housebroken easily, given the chance. If a mistake should occur, and mistakes are bound to happen, wash it immediately with tepid water, followed by another rinse with water to which a few drops of vinegar have been added. A dog will return to the same place if there is any odor left, so it is important to remove all traces.

If your puppy sleeps outside, housebreaking will be even easier. Remember that the puppy has to relieve himself after meals and whenever he wakes up, as well as sometimes in between. So take him outside as soon as he shows signs of restlessness indoors, and stay with him until he has performed. Then praise and pat him, and bring him back inside as a reward. Since he is used to taking care of himself outdoors, he will not want to misbehave in the house and will soon let you know when he wants to go out.

You can combine indoor paper training and outdoor housebreaking by taking the puppy out when convenient and keeping newspaper available for use at other times. As the puppy grows older he will be able to control himself for longer periods. If he starts to misbehave in the house,

Housebreaking demands a regular routine, and the necessary training can be made easier by using the different housebreaking aids that are sold. Scented pads, for example, serve to train a young pup. The long-handled tool shown here is excellent for picking up fecal matter in an outdoor run.

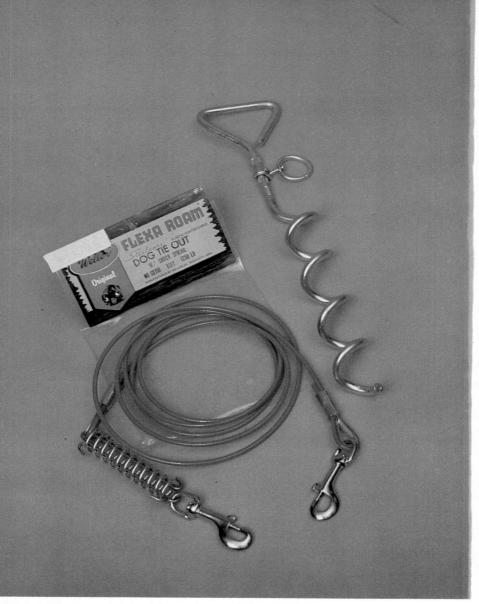

A corkscrew is an interesting piece of equipment which you can install on your property as an anchor for a long leash for your dog. Also available at pet shops is a dog trolley, which comes in various lengths and is quite useful for tying a dog outside. Always use a buckled collar, however, on your dog when you attach him to this type of equipment.

without asking to go out first, scold him and take him out or to his paper. Punishment *after* the fact will accomplish nothing; the puppy cannot understand why he is being scolded unless it is immediate.

The older puppy or grown dog should be able to remain overnight in the house without needing to go out, unless he is ill. If your dog barks or acts restless, take him out once, but unless he relieves himself right away, take him back indoors and shut him in his quarters. No dog will soil his bed if he can avoid it, and your pet will learn to control himself overnight if he must.

VETERINARY CARE

To keep your dog protected as much as possible from major diseases, maintain a routine series of inoculations.

Distemper

Young dogs are most susceptible to distemper, although it may affect dogs of all ages. Signs of the disease are loss of appetite, depression, chills, and fever, as well as a watery discharge from the eyes and nose. Unless treated promptly, the disease goes into advanced stages with infections of the lungs, intestines, and nervous system. Dogs that recover may be impaired with paralysis, convulsions, a twitch, or some other defect, usually spastic in nature. Early inoculations in puppyhood should be followed by an annual booster to help protect against this disease.

Hepatitis

The initial symptoms of hepatitis are drowsiness, vomiting, loss of appetite, high temperature, and great thirst. Often these symptoms are accompanied by swellings of the head, neck, and abdomen. This disease strikes quickly, and death may occur in only a few hours. An annual booster shot is needed after the initial series of puppy shots.

Leptospirosis

Infection is begun by the dog's licking substances contaminated by the urine or feces of infected animals, and the disease is carried by bacteria that live in stagnant or slow-moving water. The symptoms are diarrhea and a yellowish-brownish discoloration of the jaws, teeth, and tongue, caused by an inflammation of the kidneys. A veterinarian can administer the leptospirosis shot along with the distemper and hepatitis shot.

Rabies

This disease of the dog's central nervous system spreads by infectious saliva which is transmitted by the bite of an infected animal. Of the two main classes of symptoms, the first is "furious rabies," in which the dog shows a period of melancholy or depression, then irritation, and finally paralysis. The first period can be from a few hours to several days, and during this time the dog is cross and will change his position often, lose his appetite, begin to lick, and bite or swallow foreign objects. During this phase the dog is spasmodically wild and has impulses to run away. The dog acts fearless and bites everything in sight. If he is caged or confined, he will fight at the bars and possibly break teeth or fracture his jaw. His bark becomes a peculiar howl. In the final stage, the animal's lower jaw becomes paralyzed and hangs down. He then walks with a stagger, and saliva drips from his mouth. About four to eight days after the onset of paralysis, the dog dies.

The second class of symptoms is referred to as "dumb rabies" and is characterized by the dog's walking in a bearlike manner with his head down. The lower jaw is paralyzed and the dog is unable to bite. It appears as if he has a bone caught in his throat.

If a dog is bitten by a rabid animal, he probably can be saved if he is taken to a veterinarian in time for a series of injections. After the symptoms appear, however, no cure is

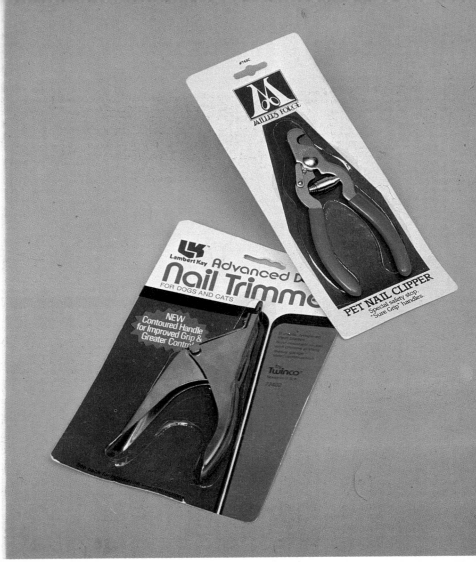

Periodic attention should be given to the claws. If allowed to grow long, the claws can cause the feet to spread and can prevent the dog from standing up on its toes properly. Also, long claws actually can grow around in a circle and back into the dog, which has a crippling arthritic effect. Specially designed nail trimmers can be purchased at pet stores. These instruments are excellent for cutting the nails in the right place and not harming the quick, which could cause pain. Only the tips, the hook-like part of the claws, should be removed on a regular basis.

An array of helpful tools on the market aids in enhancing the health, cleanliness, and appearance of a dog. Daily attention to grooming reduces the chances of parasitic skin troubles and assists in the circulation of natural oils in the coat. Such attention is appreciated by the dog and strengthens the bonds of loyalty.

possible. The local health department must be notified in the case of a rabid dog, for this is a danger to all who come near him. As with the other shots each year, an annual rabies inoculation is very important.

Parvovirus

This relatively new virus is a contagious disease that has spread in almost epidemic proportions throughout certain sections of the United States. Also, it has appeared in Australia, Canada, and Europe. Canine parvovirus attacks the intestinal tract, white blood cells, and heart muscle. It is believed to spread through dog-to-dog contact, and the specific course of infection seems to come from fecal matter of infected dogs. Overcoming parvovirus is difficult, for it is capable of existing in the environment for many months under varying conditions and temperatures, and it can be transmitted from place to place on the hair and feet of infected dogs, as well as on the clothes and shoes of people.

Vomiting and severe diarrhea, which will appear within five to seven days after the animal has been exposed to the virus, are the initial signs of this disease. At the onset of illness, feces will be light gray or yellow-gray in color, and the urine might be blood-streaked. Because of the vomiting and severe diarrhea, the dog that has contracted the disease will dehydrate quickly. Depression and loss of appetite, as well as a rise in temperature, can accompany the other symptoms. Death caused by this disease usually occurs within 48 to 72 hours following the appearance of the symptoms. Puppies are hardest hit, and the virus is fatal to 75 percent of puppies that contact it. Death in puppies can be within two days of the onset of the illness.

A series of shots administered by a veterinarian is the best preventive measure for canine parvovirus. It is also important to disinfect the area where the dog is housed by using one part sodium hypochlorite solution (household bleach) to thirty parts of water and to keep the dog from coming into contact with the fecal matter of other dogs.

INTERNAL PARASITES

Four common internal parasites that may infect a dog are: roundworms, hookworms, whipworms, and tapeworms. The first three can be diagnosed by laboratory examination, and tapeworms can be determined by seeing segments in the stool or attached to the hair around the tail. When a veterinarian determines what type of worm or worms are present, he then can advise the best treatment. A dog in good physical condition is less susceptible to worm infestation than a weak dog. Proper sanitation and a nutritious.diet help in preventing worms. One of the best preventive measures is to have clean, dry bedding for the dog, for this diminishes the possibility of reinfection due to flea or tick bites.

Heartworm infestation in dogs is passed by mosquitoes. Dogs with this disease tire easily, have difficulty in breathing, and lose weight despite a hearty appetite. Administration of preventive medicine throughout the spring, summer, and fall months is advised. A veterinarian must first take a blood sample from the dog to test for the presence of the disease, and if the dog is heartworm-free, pills or liquid medicine can be prescribed to protect against any infestation.

THE FEMALE PUPPY

If you want to spay your female, you can have it done while she is still a puppy. Her first seasonal period may occur as early as six months. She may be spayed before or after this, or you may breed her and later spay her.

The first sign of the female's being in season is a thin red discharge, which will increase for about a week, when it changes color to a thin yellowish stain, lasting about another week. Simultaneously there is a swelling of the vulva, the dog's external sexual organ. The second week is the crucial period, when she could be bred if you wanted her to have puppies, but it is possible for the period to be

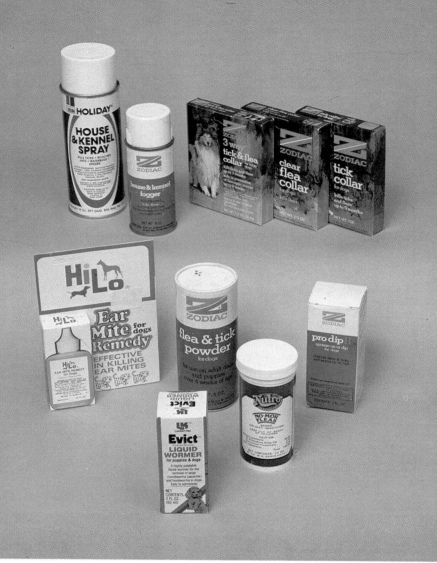

External parasites multiply rapidly, and immediate precautions should be taken if a flea, tick, or mite selects a dog as a host. Powders, foggers, dips, sprays, collars, and other remedies are helpful preventives against infestation. Not only the animal but also the entire surrounding area should be kept free of parasites.

All types of shampoo are available in pet shops. The liquid form may be medicated, conditioned, colored, reinforced against fleas or ticks, or softened. The dry shampoo is particularly appropriate in cold weather when you wish to clean a dog's coat.

shorter or longer, so it is best not to take unnecessary risks at any time. After a third week the swelling decreases and the period is over for about six months.

The female will probably lose her puppy coat, or at least shed out part of it, about three months after she is in season, for this is the time when her puppies would be weaned, if she had been mated, and females generally drop coat at that time.

If you have an absolutely climb-proof and dig-proof run, within your yard, it will be safe to leave her there, but otherwise the female in season should be shut indoors. Don't leave her out alone for even a minute; she should be exercised only on leash. If you want to prevent the neighborhood dogs from hanging around your doorstep, as they inevitably will as soon as they discover that your female is in season, take her some distance away from the house before you let her relieve herself. Take her to a near-by park or field in the car for a chance to stretch her legs. After the three weeks are up you can let her out as before, with no worry that she can have puppies until the next season. But if you want to have her spayed, consult your veterinarian about the time and age at which he prefers to do it. With a young dog the operation is simple and after a night or two at the animal hospital she can be at home. Her stitches will heal in a relatively short time, and when they are removed, you will hardly notice her souvenir scar of the routine operation. Once she has been spayed, she no longer will be able to have a litter of puppies.

4. Caring for Your Adult Dog

When your dog reaches his first birthday he is no longer a puppy, although he will not be fully mature and developed until he is two. For all intents and purposes, however, he may be considered full-grown and adult now.

DIET

You may prefer to continue feeding your dog twice a day, although he can now eat all that he needs to be healthy at one meal a day. Usually it is best to feed that one meal, or the main meal, in the evening. Most dogs eat better this way, and digest their food better. If your dog skips an occasional meal, don't worry; after half an hour remove the food if he turns up his nose at it. Otherwise he will develop the habit of picking at his food, and food left out too long becomes stale or spoiled. If you use the dry self-feeding method, of course this does not apply.

The best indication of the correct amount to feed your dog is his state of health. A fat dog is not a healthy one; just like a fat person, he has to strain his heart—and his whole body—to carry excess weight. If you cannot give your dog more exercise, cut down on his food, and remember that those dog biscuits fed as snacks or rewards count in the calories. If your dog is thin, increase the amount and add a little more fat. You can also add flavoring he likes to pep up his appetite.

NOSE, TEETH, EARS AND EYES

Normally a dog's nose, teeth, ears and eyes need no special care. The dog's nose is cool and moist to the touch (unless he has been in a warm house); however, the "cold nose" theory is only a partial indication of health or sickness. A fever, for instance, would be shown by a hot, dry nose, but other illness might not cause this. The dog's eyes are normally bright and alert, with the eyelid down in the corner, not over the eye. If the haw is bloodshot or partially covers the eye, it may be a sign of illness, or irritation. If your dog has matter in the corners of the eyes, bathe with a mild eye wash; obtain ointment from your veterinarian or pet shop to treat a chronic condition.

Your pet shop carries a variety of dishes for your dog. Bowls come in different colors, different sizes, and different weights. A dog readily recognizes his own dish and knows when it is mealtime. Remember that what a dog eats is reflected in his well-being, and there is a major difference between being "fed" and being "nourished."

A variety of water bowls can be found in pet shops. The stainless steel type comes in different capacities, such as 1 quart, 2 quarts, etc. Some types can be attached to the side of a run instead of placed on the floor or the ground; another type that is convenient is the automatic watering dish.

If your dog seems to have something wrong with his ears which causes him to scratch at them or shake his head, cautiously probe the ear with a cotton swab. An accumulation of wax will probably work itself out. But dirt or dried blood is indicative of ear mites or infection, and should be treated immediately. Sore ears in the summer, due to fly bites, should be washed with mild soap and water, then covered with a soothing ointment, gauze-wrapped if necessary. Keep the dog protected from insects, inside if necessary, until his ears heal.

YOUR DOG NEEDS TO CHEW

Puppies and young dogs need something with resistance to chew on while their teeth and jaws are developing—for cutting the puppy teeth, to induce growth of the permanent teeth under the puppy teeth, to assist in getting rid of the puppy teeth at the proper time, to help the permanent teeth through the gums, to assure normal jaw development and to settle the permanent teeth solidly in the jaws.

The adult dog's desire to chew stems from the instinct for tooth cleaning effect, gum massage and jaw exercise—plus the need for an outlet for periodic doggie tensions. In the veterinarian's book *"Canine Behavior"* published by *"Canine Practice"* Journal, Dr. Victoria L. Voith writes: "To reduce the dog's anxiety when left alone he should also be given a safety outlet such as a toy to play with and chew on. In fact, the dog may be encouraged to develop an oral attachment to this object by playing catch or tug of war with the toy at other times. Indestructible meat-flavored nylon bones are excellent."

Dental caries as it affects the teeth of humans is virtually unknown in dogs—but tartar accumulates on the teeth of dogs, particularly at the gum line, more rapidly than on the teeth of humans. These accumulations, if not removed, bring irritation, and then infection which erodes the tooth enamel and ultimately destroys the teeth at the roots. Most

52

chewing by adult dogs is an effort to do something about this problem for themselves.

Tooth and jaw development will normally continue until your dog is more than a year old—but sometimes much longer, depending upon the breed, chewing exercise, the rate at which calcium can be utilized and many other factors, known and unknown, which affect the development of individual dogs. Diseases, like distemper for example, may sometimes arrest development of the teeth and jaws, which may resume months, or even years, later.

This is why dogs, especially puppies and young dogs, will often destroy property worth hundreds of dollars, when their chewing instinct is not diverted from their owner's possessions, particularly during the widely varying critical period for young dogs.

Saving your possessions from destruction—assuring proper development of teeth and jaws—providing for 'interim' tooth cleaning and gum massage—and channeling doggie tensions into a non-destructive outlet—are, therefore, all dependent upon your dog having something suitable for chewing readily available when his instinct tells him to chew. If your purposes, and those of your dog, are to be accomplished, what you provide for chewing must be desirable from the doggie viewpoint, have the necessary functional qualities, and above all, be safe.

It is very important that dogs not be permitted to chew on anything they can break, or indigestible things from which they can bite sizeable chunks. Sharp pieces, from such as a bone which can be broken by a dog, may pierce the intestine wall and kill. Indigestible things which can be bitten off in chunks, such as toys made of rubber compound or cheap plastic, may cause an intestinal stoppage, if not regurgitated—to bring painful death, unless expensive surgery is promptly performed.

Strong natural bones, such as 4 to 8 inch lengths of round shin bone from mature beef—either the kind you can get

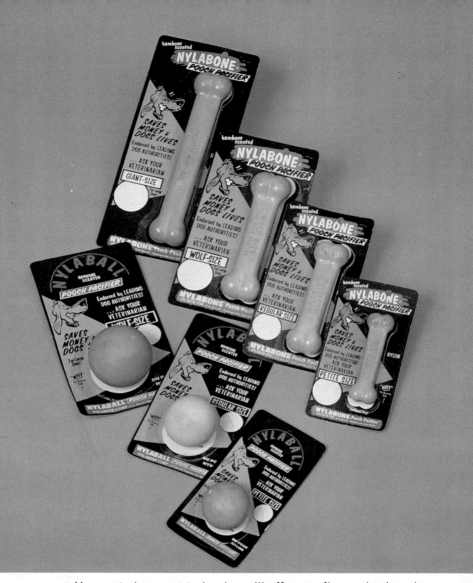

Your pet shop or veterinarian will offer you flavored-nylon chews ideally produced for dogs. Balls and bones of different sizes are recommended by many veterinarians as puppy pacifiers as well as aids in the proper development of the dog's teeth. If your dog rejects the nylon bone because of the flavor, try cooking it for 15 minutes in chicken broth, or let it soak in his regular wet food for a few hours. If your dog chews up the bones in a few months, get the next larger size.

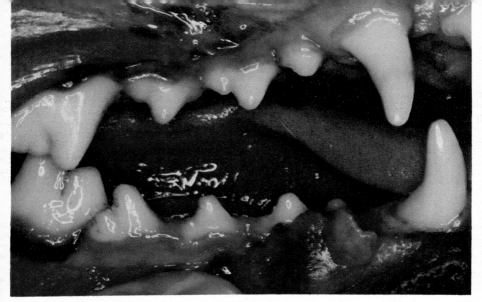

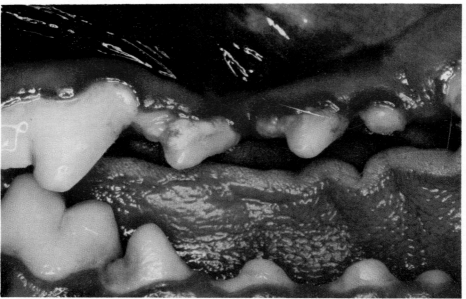

Comparison photographs of teeth and gums in dogs. *Upper photo:* Gums appear healthy and tooth surfaces are relatively clean. *Lower photo:* Gums are moderately to severely inflamed and abundant plaque and calculus are present. Photos courtesy Dr. J. Hock, School of Dental Medicine, University of Connecticut.

from your butcher or one of the variety available commercially in pet stores—may serve your dog's teething needs, if his mouth is large enough to handle them effectively.

You may be tempted to give your puppy a smaller bone and he may not be able to break it at that time—but puppies grow rapidly and the power of their jaws constantly increases until maturity. This means that a growing dog may break one of the smaller bones at any time, swallow the pieces and die painfully before you realize what is wrong.

Many people make the mistake of thinking of their dog's teeth in terms of the teeth of the wild carnivores or those of the dogs of antiquity. The teeth of the wild carnivorous animals, and the teeth found in the fossils of the dog-like creatures of antiquity, have far thicker and stronger enamel than those of our contemporary dogs. Nature provides over the centuries only that which the animal needs to survive and procreate—and dogs have been domesticated for many thousands of years.

All hard natural bones are highly abrasive. If your dog is an avid chewer, natural bones may wear away his teeth prematurely; hence, they then should be taken away from your dog when the teething purposes have been served. The badly worn, and usually painful, teeth of many mature dogs can be traced to excessive chewing on natural bones.

Nylon bones, especially those with natural meat and bone fractions added, are probably the most complete, safe and economical answer to the chewing need. Dogs cannot break them or bite off sizeable chunks; hence, they are completely safe—and being longer lasting than other things offered for the purpose, they are economical.

Hard chewing raises little bristle-like projections on the surface of the nylon bones—to provide effective interim tooth cleaning and vigorous gum massage, much in the same way your tooth brush does it for you. The little projections are raked off and swallowed in the form of thin shavings—but the chemistry of the nylon is such that they

Nylon bones which are cooked for 12 hours under high pressure and temperatures become annealed and are very strong and tough. Un-annealed nylon is brittle and dangerous for dogs. Your dog should be able to chew on them for months before the knobs on the end are chewed down and the bone has to be replaced. The bristles raised on the end of the knobs are effective as "doggie toothbrushes."

break down in the stomach fluids and pass through without harmful effect.

The toughness of the nylon provides the strong chewing resistance needed for important jaw exercise and effective help for the teething functions—but there is no tooth wear because nylon is non-abrasive. Being inert, nylon does not support the growth of micro-organisms—and it can be washed in soap and water, or it can be sterilized by boiling or in an autoclave. Many dogs, especially those whose teeth and gums have already been ravaged with poor-diet-induced degeneration, cannot chew the almost indestructible nylon bones. Your local pet shop or veterinarian has a product (the only one presently on the market is called "Mytibone") made of softer material and which has 10% of its weight composed of real bone meal. This makes the bone softer and more palatable for the older dog who refuses the nylon bone or is unable to chew it because of the condition of its teeth and gums.

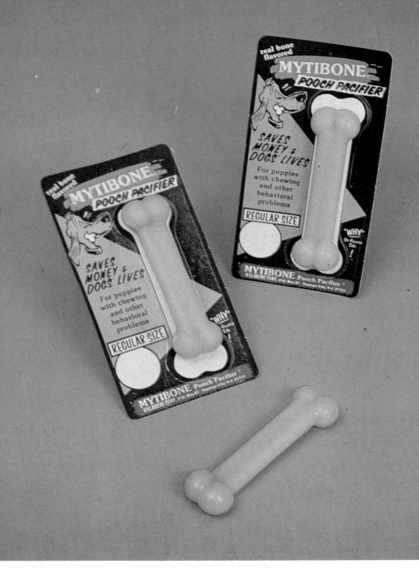

Many dogs whose teeth and jaws are such that they are unable to chew on nylon bones or balls will be attracted to products like this Mytibone in which 10% real bone meal is added before the bone is molded; addition of the bone meal makes the Mytibone softer and more chewable. This product is available only at pet shops and from your veterinarian.

...any books are available to help the dog fancier to under-
...out proper care, effective training, good grooming, first
...ases, inoculations, breeding, whelping, and canine ter-
...

Nothing, however, substitutes for periodic professional attention to your dog's teeth and gums, not any more than your toothbrush can do that for you. Have your dog's teeth cleaned by your veterinarian at least once a year; twice a year is better—and he will be healthier, happier and far more pleasant to live with.

PARASITES

Should your dog pick up fleas or other skin parasites from neighbors' dogs or from the ground, weekly use of a good anti-flea preparation (available at your pet shop) will keep them off. Remember to treat his bed and change the bedding too, as flea eggs drop off the host to hatch and wait in likely places for the dog to return. In warm weather a weekly treatment or monthly dip is good prevention.

If your grown dog is well fed and in good health you will probably have no trouble with worms. He may pick them

Fleas not only keep a dog scratching but also carry tapeworm, heartworm, and other parasites. They can exist in the bedding of the dog and can multiply rapidly. A female flea will lay her eggs, and these will become adult fleas in less than three weeks. Depending on the temperature and the amount of moisture, large numbers of fleas can attack dogs, and ears of dogs can particularly play host to hundreds of fleas. Obviously, you should keep your dog's living quarters clean.

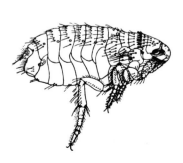
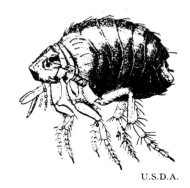

U.S.D.A.

up from other dogs, however, so if you suspect worms, have a stool examination made and, if necessary, worm him. Fleas, too, are carriers of tapeworm, so that is one good reason to make sure the dog is free from these insects. Roundworms, the dog's most common intestinal parasite, have a life cycle which permits complete eradication by worming twice, ten days apart. The first worming will remove all adults and the second will destroy all subsequently hatched eggs before they in turn can produce more parasites.

FIRST AID

Should your dog be injured, you can give him first aid which is, in general, similar to that for a human. The same principles apply. Superficial wounds should be disinfected and healing ointment applied. If the cut is likely to get dirty, apply a bandage and restrain the dog so that he won't keep trying to remove it. A cardboard ruff will prevent him from licking his chest or body. The dog's nails can be taped down to prevent scratching.

A board splint should be put on before moving a dog which might have a broken bone. If you are afraid that the dog will bite from pain, use a bandage muzzle made from a long strip of cloth, wrapped around the muzzle, then tied under the jaw and brought up behind the ears to hold it on. In case of severe bleeding apply a tourniquet—a strip of cloth wrapped around a stick to tighten it will do—between the cut on a limb and the heart, but loosen it every few minutes to avoid damaging the circulation.

If you suspect that your dog has swallowed poison, try to get him to vomit by giving him salt water or mustard in water. In all these cases, rush him to your veterinarian as soon as possible, after alerting the vet by phone.

In warm weather the most important thing to remember for your dog's sake is providing fresh water. If he tends to

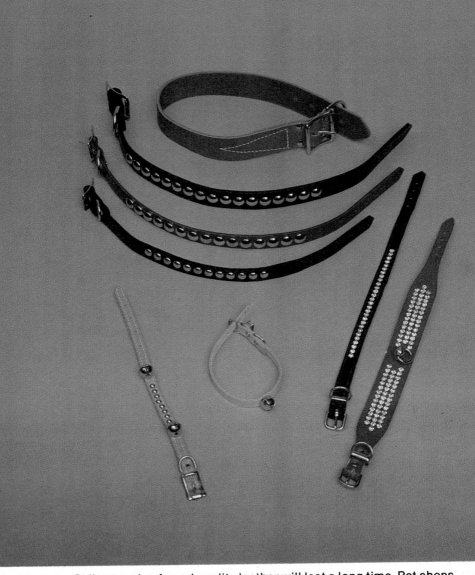

Collars made of good quality leather will last a long time. Pet shops carry a wide variety of collars to suit every taste; just make sure that the collar you choose is of the proper size—and don't forget that what fits your dog when it's a puppy won't necessarily fit after the dog is fully grown.

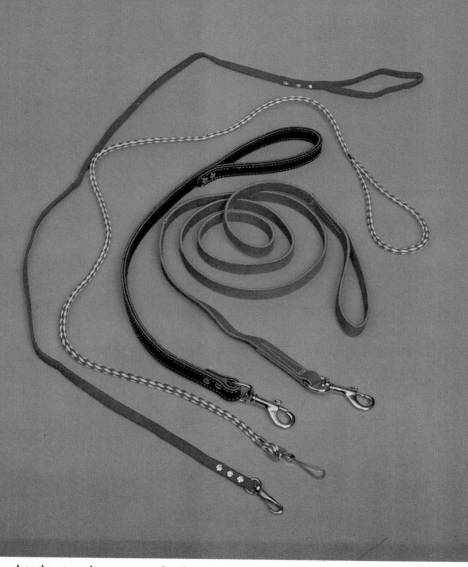

Leads come in an array of colors, widths, and lengths, as shown in
the above photo. The leather leash that is attached to a leather
collar may be color-coordinated. Most important is that the equipment be strong enough to hold the weight of the dog.

slobber and drink too much, it may be offered at intervals of an hour or so instead of being available at all times, but it should be fresh and cool. Don't over-exercise the dog or let the children play too wildly with him in the heat of the day. Don't leave him outside without shade, and never leave a dog in a car which could become overheated in the sun. The car should always be parked in the shade and provide ventilation through the windows.

THE OLD DOG

With the increased knowledge and care available, there is no reason why your dog should not live to a ripe old age. As he grows older he may need a little additional care, however. Remember that a fat dog is not healthy, particularly as he grows older, and limit his food accordingly. The older dog needs exercise as much as ever, although his heart cannot bear the strain of sudden and violent exertion. His digestion may not be as good as it was as a puppy, so follow your veterinarian's advice about special feeding, if necessary. Failing eyesight and hearing mean lessened awareness of dangers, so you must protect him more than before. The old dog is used to his home and is set in his ways, so too many strangers are bound to be a strain. For the same reason, boarding him out or a trip to the vet's is to be avoided unless absolutely necessary.

Should you decide at this time to get a puppy, to avoid being without a dog when your old retainer is no longer with you, be very careful how you introduce the puppy. He is naturally playful and will expect the older dog to respond to his advances. Sometimes the old dog will get a new lease on life from a pup. But don't make him jealous by giving to the newcomer the attention that formerly was exclusively his. Feed them apart, and show the old dog that you still love him the most; the puppy, not being used to individual attention will not mind sharing your love.

5. Breeding the Female and Raising Puppies

Whether or not you bought your female dog intending to breed her, some preparation is necessary when and if you decide to take this step.

WHEN TO BREED

It is usually best to breed on the second or third season. Plan in advance the time of year which is best for you, taking into account where the puppies will be born and raised. You will keep them until they are at least six weeks old, and a litter of pups takes up considerable space by then. Other considerations are selling the puppies (Christmas vs. springtime sales), your own vacation, and time available to care for them. You'll need at least an hour a day to feed and clean up after the mother and puppies but probably it will take you much longer—with time out to admire and play with them!

CHOOSING THE STUD

You can plan to breed your female about 6½ months after the start of her last season, although a variation of a month or two either way is not unusual. Choose the stud dog and make arrangements well in advance. If you are breeding for show stock, which may command better prices, a mate should be chosen with an eye to complementing the deficiencies of your female. If possible, they should have several ancestors in common within the last two or three generations, as such combinations generally "click" best. He should have a good show record or be the sire of show winners if old enough to be proven.

The owner of such a male usually charges a fee for the use of the dog. This does not guarantee a litter, but you generally have the right to breed your female again if she does not have puppies. In some cases the owner of the stud will agree to take a choice puppy in place of a stud fee. You should settle all details beforehand, including the possibility of a single surviving puppy, deciding the age at which he is to make his choice and take the pup, and so on.

If you want to raise a litter "just for the fun of it" and plan merely to make use of an available male, the most important selection point is temperament. Make sure the dog is friendly as well as healthy, because a bad disposition could appear in his puppies, and this is the worst of all traits in a dog destined to be a pet. In such cases a "stud fee puppy," not necessarily the choice of the litter, is the usual payment.

PREPARATION FOR BREEDING

Before you breed your female, make sure she is in good health. She should be neither too thin nor too fat. Any skin disease *must* be cured, so that it is not passed on to the puppies. If she has worms she should be wormed before being bred or within three weeks afterward. It is generally considered a good idea to revaccinate her against distemper and hepatitis before the puppies are born. This will increase the immunity the puppies receive during their early, most vulnerable period.

The female will probably be ready to breed 12 days after the first colored discharge. You can usually make arrangements to board her with the owner of the male for a few days, to insure her being there at the proper time, or you can take her to be mated and bring her home the same day. If she still appears receptive she may be bred again two days later. However, some females never show signs of willingness, so it helps to have the experience of a breeder. Usually the second day after the discharge changes color is the proper time, and she may be bred for about three days

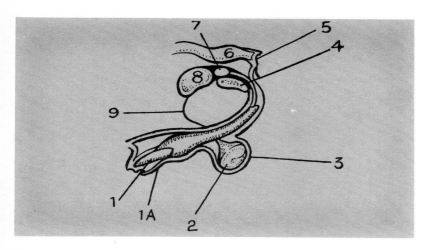

The reproductive system of a male: 1a, sheath; 1, penis; 2, testicle; 3, scrotum; 4, pelvic bone; 5, anus; 6, rectum; 7, prostate; 8, bladder; 9, vas deferens.

The reproduction system of the bitch: 1, vulva; 2, anus; 3, vagina; 4, cervix; 5, uterus; 6, ovary; 7, kidneys; 8, ribs; 9, fetal lump.

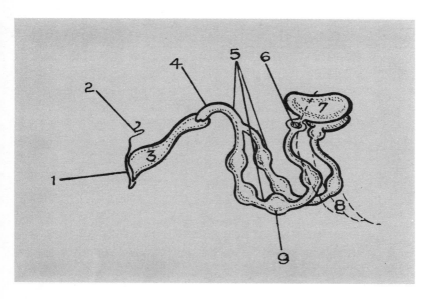

following. For an additional week or so she may have some discharge and attract other dogs by her odor, but can seldom be bred.

THE FEMALE IN WHELP

You can expect the puppies nine weeks from the day of breeding, although 61 days is as common as 63. During this time the female should receive normal care and exercise. If she was overweight, don't increase her food at first; excess weight at whelping time is bad. If she is on the thin side build her up, giving some milk and biscuit at noon if she likes it. You may add one of the mineral and vitamin supplements to her food, to make sure that the puppies will be healthy. As her appetite increases, feed her more. During the last two weeks the puppies grow enormously and she will probably have little room for food and less appetite. She should be tempted with meat, liver and milk, however.

As the female in whelp grows heavier, cut out violent exercise and jumping. Although a dog used to such activities will often play with the children or run around voluntarily, restrain her for her own sake.

An approaching sign of whelping is loss of hair around the breasts. This should be combed out, or cut if she does not shed, as it will be in the puppies' way.

PREPARING FOR THE PUPPIES

Prepare a whelping box a few days before the puppies are due, and allow the mother to sleep there overnight or to spend some time in it during the day to become accustomed to it. Then she is less likely to try to have her pups under the front porch or in the middle of your bed. A variety of places will serve such as a corner of your cellar, garage, or an unused room. If the weather is warm, a large outdoor doghouse will do, well protected from rain or draft. A whelping box serves to separate mother and puppies from visitors and other distractions. The walls should be high enough to restrain the puppies, yet allow the mother to get away from the puppies after she has fed them. Four feet square is minimum size, and one-foot walls will keep the pups in until they begin to climb, when it should be built up. Then the puppies really need more room anyway, so double the space with a very low partition down the middle and you will find them naturally housebreaking themselves.

Layers of newspapers spread over the whole area will make excellent bedding and be absorbent enough to keep the surface warm and dry. They should be removed daily and replaced with another thick layer. An old quilt or washable blanket makes better footing for the nursing puppies than slippery newspaper during the first week and is softer for the mother.

Be prepared for the actual whelping several days in advance. Usually the female will tear up papers, refuse food and generally act restless. These may be false alarms; the real test is her temperature, which will drop to below 100° about 12 hours before whelping. Take it with a rectal thermometer morning and evening, and put her in the pen, looking in on her frequently, when the temperature goes down.

WHELPING

Usually little help is needed but it is wise to stay close to make sure that the mother's lack of experience does not cause an unnecessary accident. Be ready to help when the first puppy arrives, for it could smother if she does not break the membrane enclosing it. She should start right away to lick the puppy, drying and stimulating it, but you can do it with a soft rough towel, instead. The afterbirth should follow the birth of each puppy, attached to the puppy by the long umbilical cord. Watch to make sure that each is expelled anyway, for retaining this material can cause infection. In her instinct for cleanliness the mother will probably eat the afterbirth after biting the cord. One or two will not hurt her; they stimulate milk supply as well as labor for remaining pups. But too many can make her lose appetite for the food she needs to feed her pups and regain her strength. So remove the rest of them along with the wet newspapers and keep the pen dry and clean to relieve her anxiety.

If the mother does not bite the cord, or does it too close to the body, take over the job, to prevent an umbilical hernia. Tearing is recommended, but you can cut it, about two inches from the body, with a sawing motion of scissors, sterilized in alcohol. Then dip the end in a shallow dish of iodine; the cord will dry up and fall off in a few days.

The puppies should follow each other at intervals of not more than half an hour. If more time goes past and you are sure there are still pups to come, a brisk walk outside may start labor again. If she is actively straining without producing a puppy it may be presented backward, a so-called "breech" or upside down birth. Careful assistance with a well-soaped finger to feel for the puppy or ease it back may help, but never attempt to pull it by force against the mother. This could cause serious damage, so let an expert handle it.

If anything seems wrong, waste no time in calling your veterinarian who can examine her and if necessary give hormones which will bring the remaining puppies. You may want his experience in whelping the litter even if all goes well. He will probably prefer to have the puppies born at his hospital rather than to get up in the middle of the night to come to your home. The mother would, no doubt, prefer to stay at home, but you can be sure she will get the best of care in his hospital. If the puppies are born at home and all goes as it should, watch the mother carefully afterward.

It is wise to have the veterinarian check her and the pups.

RAISING THE PUPPIES

Hold each puppy to a breast as soon as he is dry for a good meal without competition. Then he may join his littermates in the basket, out of his mother's way while she is whelping. Keep a supply of evaporated milk on hand for emergencies, or later weaning. A formula of evaporated milk, corn syrup and a little water with egg yolk should be warmed and fed in a doll or baby bottle if necessary. A supplementary feeding often helps weak pups over the hump. Keep track of birth weights, and weekly readings, thereafter; it will furnish an accurate record of the pups' growth and health.

After the puppies have arrived, take the mother outside for a walk and drink, and then leave her to take care of them. She will probably not want to stay away more than a minute or two for the first few weeks. Be sure to keep water available at all times, and feed her milk or broth frequently, as she needs liquids to produce milk. Encourage her to eat, with her favorite foods, until she asks for it of her own accord. She will soon develop a ravenous appetite and should have at least two large meals a day, with dry food available in addition.

Prepare a warm place to put the puppies after they are born to keep them dry and help them to a good start in life. An electric heating pad or hot water bottle covered with flannel in the bottom of a cardboard box should be set near the mother so that she can see her puppies. She will usually allow you to help, but don't take the puppies out of sight, and let her handle things if your interference seems to make her nervous.

Be sure that all the puppies are getting enough to eat. If the mother sits or stands instead of lying still to nurse, the probable cause is scratching from the puppies' nails. You can remedy this by clipping them, as you do hers. Manicure scissors will do for these tiny claws. Some breeders advise disposing of the smaller or weaker pups in a large litter, as the mother has trouble in handling more than six or seven. But you can help her out by preparing an extra puppy box or basket. Leave half the litter with the mother and the other half in a warm place, changing off at two hour intervals at first. Later you may change them less frequently, leaving them all together except during the day. Try supplementary feeding, too; as soon as their eyes open, at about two weeks, they will lap from a dish, anyway.

WEANING THE PUPPIES

The puppies should normally be completely weaned at five weeks, although you start to feed them at three weeks. They will find it easier to lap semi-solid food than to drink milk at first, so mix baby cereal with whole or evaporated milk, warmed to body temperature, and offer it to the puppies in a saucer. Until they learn to lap it, it is best to feed one or two at a time because they are more likely to walk into it than to eat it. Hold the saucer at chin level, and let them gather around, keeping paws out of the dish. A damp sponge afterward prevents most of the cereal from sticking to the skin if the mother doesn't clean them up. Once they have gotten the idea, broth or babies' meat soup may be alternated with milk, and you can start them on finely chopped meat. At four weeks they will eat four meals a day, and soon do without their mother entirely. Start them on mixed dog food, or leave it with them in a dish for self-feeding. Don't leave water with them all the time; at this age everything is to play with and they will use it as a wading pool. They can drink all they need if it is offered several times a day, after meals.

As the puppies grow up the mother will go into the pen only to nurse them, first sitting up and then standing. To dry her up completely, keep the mother away for longer periods; after a few days of part-time nursing she can stay away for longer periods, and then completely. The little milk left will be resorbed.

The puppies may be put outside, unless it is too cold, as soon as their eyes are open, and will benefit from the sunlight and vitamins. A rubber mat or newspapers underneath will protect them from cold or damp. At six weeks they can go outside permanently unless it is very cold but make sure that they go into their shelter at night or in bad weather. By now cleaning up is a man-sized job, so put them out at least during the day and make your task easier. Be sure to clean their run daily, as worms and other infections are lurking. You can expect the pups to need at least one worming before they are ready to go to new homes, so take a stool sample to your veterinarian before they are three weeks old. If one puppy has worms all should be wormed. Follow the veterinarian's advice, and this applies also to vaccination. If you plan to keep a pup you will want to vaccinate him at the earliest age, so his littermates should be done at the same time.

6. How to Train Your Dog

ANIMAL OR PET?

There is only a one-word difference between an *animal* and a *pet* and the word is TRAINING.

But training your dog depends upon many factors:
> how intelligent you are;
> how intelligent the dog is;
> what your intentions are;
> how much time you are willing to devote to the task.

First we consider the dog owner who is merely interested in training his dog to be a perfect home companion, a dog that he can be proud to own, a dog that won't embarrass him by untimely "accidents" nor kill himself by running into the street.

THE DOG OWNER'S PART

Before you begin training your dog to be a pet, there are certain important facts to remember:

You are a human being and do not speak the same language that a dog does. So you must try to think as a pet dog thinks; your dog will try to understand his trainer.

Training your dog is like training a child. It requires firmness tempered with kindness, strictness but gentleness, consistency, repetition and above all PATIENCE. You must have the patience to go over the training cycle time and time again until the message reaches your dog.

Did you know that a dog is the only known animal that can be bribed into learning by just a few kind words and soft pats on the back? Other animals must be bribed with food or be beaten into submission, but not your pet dog. He wants kindness and attention. Reward him with a pat on the back when he is doing well and you will soon have a dog eager to learn.

You can easily train your dog to become a well-behaved member of your family. Training should begin the day you get him. Although a puppy under six months is too young to expect much of in the way of obedience, you should teach him to respect your authority. Be consistent. Don't allow the pup to jump all over you when you are wearing old clothes, because you can't expect him to know the difference when you are dressed for a party. Don't encourage the dog to climb into your lap or onto your bed, then punish him for leaving hair on furniture when you aren't around. Although six months to a year is the best time to begin serious training, a dog of any age can learn if taught with consideration and patience. You *can* teach an old dog new tricks.

Housebreaking has already been covered. You cannot expect perfection from a puppy, or even an older dog, particularly if he is not used to living in a house. Going into a strange place, a dog is likely to be ill at ease and make a mistake for that reason. Remember that once it has happened, the only way to prevent further accidents is to avoid the opportunity and to be sure to remove traces which would remind the dog of previous errors.

It is a convenience when traveling to be able to keep him on leash, so take the time to teach him before it is necessary. "Curb your dog" is the rule in most cities; for the sake of others you should teach your dog to obey it.

GIVING COMMANDS

When you give commands use the shortest phrase possible and use the same word with the same meaning at all times. If you want to teach your dog to sit, then always use the word SIT. If you want your dog to lie down, then always use the word DOWN. It doesn't matter what word you use as long as your dog becomes accustomed to hearing it and acts upon it.

The trick-trained dog that always sits on the command UP and stands on the command SIT was easily trained to understand the words that way. The words are merely sounds to him. He cannot understand you but he understands the tone of your voice and the inflection of the words.

Unless you are consistent in your use of commands you can never train your animal properly.

WHAT ABOUT LESSONS?

Try to make your training lessons interesting and appealing both to yourself and your dog. Short frequent lessons are of much more value than long lessons. It is much better for all concerned if you teach your dog for 10 minutes at a time, three times a day, than for 30 minutes once a day. The 10 minute session amuses both you and your dog and the attachment which develops between you during these lessons will be everlasting.

A good time to train your dog is for 10 minutes before you give him his breakfast; then he assumes that the meal is a reward for his being such a good dog. If you follow this schedule for all three meals your training program will be extremely successful.

WHAT YOU WILL TEACH YOUR DOG

Your house pet should certainly learn the rudiments necessary to good behavior. Your dog should be housebroken first of all. Then he should learn how to walk properly with a collar and leash, after which he should be taught the simple commands of HEEL, SIT, COME and STAY. Only after the dog has learned these commands is it safe to train him off the leash.

Once your dog gets into the swing of his training it is wise to continue to train him in more difficult performances. After all, the hardest part of the job is establishing a communication system so that each of you learns what to expect from the other. Once your dog learns a trick or a command he will hardly ever forget it if you repeat it every so often. Begging, giving his paw, playing dead and rolling over, are entertaining tricks which you, your friends and your dog can all enjoy to mutual benefit. There are, however, more important lessons first.

COLLAR AND LEASH

Your puppy should become used to a leash and collar at an early age. He seldom needs a license until he is six months old, and a leather collar will be outgrown several times before then. Buy one for use, not looks or permanence. A thin chain "choke collar" is a good substitute, but you will want a larger and slightly heavier one for training later on. Never leave a choke on a loose dog, for it could catch on something and strangle him. If you want to use one as a permanent collar, buy a clip to fasten the two ends, so that it cannot choke him.

The correct way to put a choke chain on a dog is to have the longer end (which is through the loop) go across the top (toward the left) of the dog's head. The lead then is attached to the longer end.

Let the puppy wear his collar around until he is used to its feel and weight. After several short periods he will not be distracted by the strangeness and you can attach the leash. Let him pull it around and then try to lead him a bit. He will probably resist, bucking and balking, or simply sit down and refuse to budge. Fight him for a few minutes, dragging him along if necessary, but then let him relax for the day, with plenty of affection and praise. He won't be lead-broken until he learns that he must obey the pull under any circumstance, but don't try to do it in one lesson. Ten minutes a day is long enough for any training. The dog's period of concentration is short and, like a child, he will become bored if you carry it on too long.

TRAINING YOUR DOG TO WALK PROPERLY

After your dog has been housebroken and has become accustomed to his collar or harness you must teach him to walk properly on a leash. We are assuming that you will use the collar and leash when housebreaking your puppy. Once he is thoroughly familiar with the workings of these restraining objects, you must teach him to respect the master at the other end of the leash.

You should hold the leash firmly in your right hand. The dog should walk on your left side with the leash crossing the front of your body. The reason for this will be obvious once you've actually walked your dog . . . you have more control this way.

Let your dog lead you for the first few moments so that he fully understands that freedom can be his if he goes about it properly. He knows already that when he wants to go outdoors the leash and collar are necessary, so he has respect for the leash. Now, if while walking, he starts to pull in one direction all you do is *stop walking*. He will walk a few steps and then find that he can't walk any further. He will then turn and look into your face. *This is the crucial point*. Just stand there for a moment and stare right back at him . . . Now walk another ten feet and stop again. Again your dog will probably walk out the leash, find he can't go any further, and turn around and look again. If he starts to pull and jerk then just stand there. After he quiets down, just bend down and comfort him as he may be frightened. Keep up this training until he learns not to outwalk you.

Once the puppy obeys the pull of the leash half your training is accomplished. "Heeling" is a necessity for a well-behaved dog, so teach him to walk beside you, head even with your knee. Nothing looks sadder than a big dog taking his helpless owner for a walk. It is annoying to passers-by and other dog owners to have a large dog, however friendly, bear down on them and entangle dogs, people and packages.

To teach your dog, start off walking briskly, saying "Heel" in a firm voice. Pull back with a sharp jerk if he lunges ahead, and if he lags repeat the command and tug on the leash, not allowing him to drag behind. After the dog has learned to heel at various speeds on leash, you can remove it and practice heeling free, but have it ready to snap on again as soon as he wanders.

You must understand that most dogs like to stop and sniff around a bit until they find THE place to do their duty. Be kind enough to stop and wait when they find it necessary to pause. This is the whole story . . . it's as easy as that. A smart dog can learn to walk properly in a few days, provided you have taught him correctly from the beginning. A dog that is incorrectly trained initially may take a month to retrain, but in any event, every dog can learn to walk properly on a leash!

TEACHING YOUR DOG TO COME, SIT AND STAY

When the dog understands the pull of the leash he should learn to come. Never call him to you for punishment, or he will be quick to disobey. (Always go to him if he has been disobedient.) To teach him to come, let him reach the end of a long lead, then give the command, pulling him toward you at the same time. As soon as he associates the word "Come" with the action, pull only when he does not respond immediately. As he starts to come, back up to make him learn that he must come from a distance as well as when he is close to you. Soon you can practice without a leash, but if he is slow to come or actively disobedient, go to him and pull him toward you, repeating the command. More practice with leash on is needed.

Your dog has been named and he knows his name. After hearing his name called over and over again in your home, he finds that it pays to come when called. Why? Because you only call him when his food is ready or when you wish to play with him and pet him. Outside the house it is a different story. He would rather play by himself or with other dogs or chase a cat than play with you. So, he must be trained to come to you when he is called.

"Sit," "Down," and "Stay" are among the most useful commands and will make it easier for you to control your dog on many occasions—when grooming him, when he needs veterinary care, out walking if you meet a strange dog, or in the car, to mention a few. Teaching him to sit is the first step. With collar and leash on have him stand in the "Heel" position. Give the command, "Sit," at the same time pulling up on the leash in your right hand and pressing down on his hindquarters with your left. As soon as he sits, release the pressure and praise him.

To teach your dog to stay, bring your hand close to his face with a direct motion, at the same time as you give the order. Ask him to remain only a few seconds at first, but gradually the time can be increased and you can leave him at a distance. If he should move, return immediately and make him sit and stay again, after scolding him.

TRAINING YOUR DOG TO STOP WITHOUT COMMAND

When your dog has been trained to HEEL on a loose leash, the next step in his training is to STOP without command so that if you stop for a street corner or to talk to someone along the way, your dog doesn't pull you to get going. Training to stop without command requires use of the choke chain collar for the first lessons.

Take your dog out for his usual walk, keeping him at HEEL all the time. Then stop dead in your tracks keeping the leash tight in your hands without a bit of slack. DO NOT LET HIM SIT DOWN! No command is necessary. As soon as he stops, pat him on the back and give him some dog candy. Then walk on again briskly and stop short. Keep your dog on the tight leash at all times and repeat this until he learns that he must stop dead in his tracks just as you do. When you stop, stop *deliberately* so that he can actually anticipate your stopping and be with you at all times. You can tell when he is being attentive for he will walk a few steps and then turn his head so that he can keep an eye on your face. He will actually crave to satisfy you once he has been properly taught, and he will only take a few steps before he swings his head to look at you. Next time you see a well-trained dog walking along the street, notice how much time he spends looking at his master instead of at other things.

Once your dog has learned to stop without command and you want to walk again, you can signal him by many means. One way is to slacken your leash and then start walking so that he will learn that a slackened leash means you intend to walk again. Another way is to signal him verbally with the word "Go" or "Come on, Pal" or something similar to that. It doesn't matter what word you use as long as you use the same word all the time.

OFF-THE-LEASH TRAINING

After your dog has accomplished these lessons it is time to begin his training without a leash. Try to find a large open area which is fenced in. It will be safer to advance to this stage within the confines of that area. If no such area is available, find as quiet a street as you can (even late at night so that few automobiles are around) and begin your training there.

Let's assume that your dog heels and stops without command. After you've walked him a few feet and tested him on stopping without command, bend down and remove the leash. Start walking briskly as you did when training him to heel. Stop suddenly without command and see if he does the same. If he doesn't, then immediately snap on the leash with the choke collar and go through the training again. Walk once with the leash on and once with the leash off, until finally your dog gets the idea that he can have more freedom by behaving himself, than misbehaving. Don't forget to carry some dog candy along with you so you can reward him for a successful performance.

It is important for you and your dog to use his regular collar during "off-training" hours, since your dog likes a recess every few days. Then when you put on the training collar he knows that something new is coming along. Every time you put on the training collar give him a piece of candy and an extra pat or two. Let him know that both of you are going to enjoy the new experience.

TRAINING YOUR DOG TO LIE DOWN

To teach your dog to lie down, have him sit facing you. Pull down on the leash by putting your foot on it and pulling at the same time as you say "Down." Gesture toward the ground with a sweep of your arm. When he begins to understand what is wanted, do it without the leash and alternate voice and hand signals. Teach him to lie down from standing as well as sitting position, and begin to do it from a distance. Hand signals are particularly useful when your dog can see you but is too far away to hear, and they may be used in teaching all commands.

When giving the hand signal be careful that your dog doesn't think you are threatening him. You can dispel this fear by immediately offering him some dog candy each time he successfully completes the lying down maneuver.

DISCIPLINE TRAINING FOR YOUR DOG

Up to this point you have been training your dog to act upon command. Now you will attempt to train his intelligence. This is another important part of the training problem and it is the part that separates a "smart" dog from one that doesn't "use his head."

All dogs, regardless of their training, will get the urge to run after another dog, to chase a cat, to fetch, or just to run for the sheer love of running. In the open field or park this is perfectly all right, but in the city it can be catastrophic! Let's assume that your dog has a bad habit of slipping off his collar and making a mad dash away from you. You may find this out some fine, bright morning when both of you are in fine spirits: he will spot a cat, and without warning will dash off, either pulling the leash right out of your unwary hands or slipping his head out of the collar. A moment of panic will hit you both. But, once the inital impact of the moment is over, he will come scampering back at the command COME.

At this point do not beat your dog. He knows he has done something wrong and he is a bit confused himself. Just pat him on the head and ignore it . . . *this time.* Then walk back to the house and get a long rope, 25 to 30 feet long. Tie this rope to his regular collar (do not use a choke chain) and also use the regular leash. Try to get your dog into the same situation as the one he bolted from. When he runs away from you again (if he does), drop the leash but hold onto the rope. When he gets far enough away give a loud holler STOP and jerk the rope at the same time. He will spin in his tracks and lay where he is, thoroughly confused and a bit scared.

Go over to him and make a big fuss over him as though you can't imagine what happened. Tell him he should never have left your side. Repeat this training four or five times and he will never bolt from you again.

You can practice the command STOP by running a few steps with him and then shouting the command STOP as you suddenly stop short. By repeating the command STOP in every such situation it won't be too long before you can make your dog STOP on a dime!

TRAINING YOUR DOG NOT TO JUMP ON PEOPLE

Some dogs are so affectionate that they will jump on everybody who comes into sight in order to get their attention and affection. Only you can train your dog not to jump and it's an easy trick to learn. As he jumps up to greet *you,* merely bend your knee so he hits it with his chest and falls over. He cannot see your knee coming up as his head will be above your knee. After a few falls he will get the idea that it isn't practical to jump up to greet you or anyone.

Of course if he has learned the meaning of the command DOWN, then use that command when he jumps up. He won't like to assume the down position when he is anxious for a pat or piece of dog candy, so this will be an easy lesson for him to learn.

KEEPING YOUR DOG OFF THE FURNITURE

Your favorite sofa or chair will also be your dog's favorite seat. It is naturally used the most and so will have the odors (which only your dog can smell) of the beloved master. There are two ways of training your dog out of the habit of sitting in your chair. (You will want to break the habit because most dogs shed and their hair gets all over your clothes. Then again, he might like to curl up in your lap while you are trying to read or knit.)

The simplest way of breaking the habit is to soak a small rag with a special dog scent which is repulsive to dogs. Put the rag on the chair which your dog favors. He will jump on the chair, get a whiff of the scent and make a detour of the chair forever more!

Another way to train is to pull him off the chair every time you catch him there and immediately command him to lie DOWN at your feet. Then give him a severe tongue lashing. After a few times he will never go to the chair again WHILE YOU ARE AROUND! The greater problem is to teach him to stay away all the time. The usual plan is to get a few inexpensive mouse traps and set them (without bait of course) with a few sheets of newspaper over them. As soon as your dog jumps onto the chair the mousetrap goes SNAP and off the chair goes the dog. He may try it again, but then the second trap will go off, and he will have learned his lesson.

Since your dog has his own bed, train him to stay in it when you don't want him to be any place else. This can be done by saying the word BED in a loud voice and dragging him over and placing him in it. Do this a few times and he will learn where to go when you want him in bed!

TRAINING YOUR DOG TO DO TRICKS

Nearly every housedog learns a few tricks without training during the course of his puppyhood. These are usually accidentally learned, but the master observes the dog doing them and then prompts him to repeat the same thing over and over again.

You will deliberately want to train your dog to shake hands. First get him into the sitting position. Then upon the command PAW, lift his paw in your hand and shake it vigorously without knocking him off balance. Then give him a piece of dog candy. Repeat this several times a day and in a week he will all but hold out his paw when you walk in the door!

Teaching your dog to beg is done in the same manner. Place him in the sitting position with the proper command. Then lift his front paws up until he is in a begging position. Hold him that way until he finds a comfortable balance and then let him balance himself. As he gets his balance, hold a piece of dog candy right over his nose. As soon as you let go of his front paws, lower the dog candy to his mouth and let him take it from your hands. Hold the dog candy firmly so it takes a few seconds for him to pry it loose, during this time you are saying BEG, over and over. From then on, you must bribe him with dog candy until he assumes the begging position upon the command BEG. Repeat the preliminary training until he eagerly goes into the begging position to earn dog candy.

TRAINING YOUR DOG TO RETRIEVE

Most dogs are born retrievers and their natural instinct is to chase something that moves. First go to a pet shop and pick out a rubber toy. Try a rubber ball, a rubber bone, anything that attracts your eye. They are all made of completely harmless rubber and are safe even if your dog chews them up.

Then take your dog outside and throw the toy a few feet. He will usually chase it and pick it up. If he doesn't, then you must walk him over to the toy and place it in his mouth and walk him back to your starting position with it. Repeat this operation until he learns the game. Once he goes after the toy, call him to you. If he drops it along the way merely send him back for it by pointing to the object. If necessary, walk him back to the toy, put it in his mouth and walk back with him to the original starting position. When he successfully brings back the object you can reward him with a piece of dog candy.

7. Showing Your Dog

As your puppy grows he will doubtless have many admirers among your friends, some of whom are bound to say, "Oh, what a handsome dog—you should certainly show him!" Perhaps even a breeder or judge will say he has show possibilities, and although you didn't buy him with that thought in mind, "Cinderella" champions do come along now and then—often enough to keep dog breeders perennially optimistic.

If you do have ideas of showing your dog, get the opinion of someone with experience first. With favorable criticism, go ahead making plans to show him. For the novice dog and handler, match shows are a good way to gain ring poise and experience. These are small shows often held by the local kennel club or breed specialty club, found in many cities. Entry fees are low and paid at the door, breeds and sexes are usually judged together, and the prizes and ribbons are not important. They provide a good opportunity to learn what goes on at a show, and to conquer ring nervousness. Matches are usually held during the evening or on a weekend afternoon, and you need stay only to be judged.

Before you go to a show your dog should be trained—to gait at a trot beside you, with head up and in a straight line. In the ring you will have to gait around the edge with other dogs and then individually up and down the center runner. In addition the dog must stand for examination by the

DOG SHOW JUDGING PROCEDURE

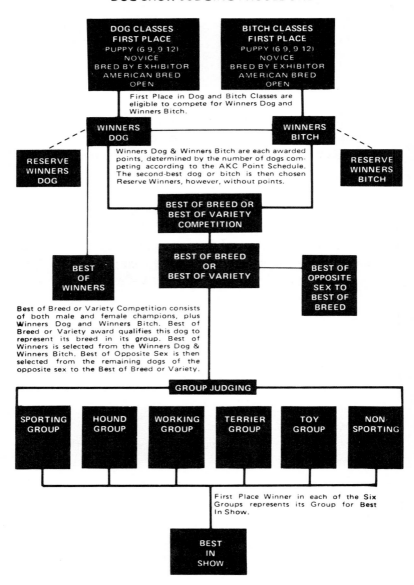

judge, who will look at him closely and feel his head and body structure. He should be taught to stand squarely, hind feet slightly back, head up on the alert. He must hold the pose when you place his feet and show animation for a piece of boiled liver in your hand or a toy mouse thrown in front of you.

ADVANCE PREPARATION

The day before the benched point show, pack your kit. You will want to take a water dish and bottle of water for your dog (so that he won't be affected by a change in drinking water, and you won't have to go look for it). A chain or leash to fasten him to the bench, or stall, where he must remain during the show, and a show lead should be included, as well as grooming tools. The show lead is a thin nylon or cord collar and leash combined, which detracts from the dog's appearance less than a clumsier chain and lead. Also put in the identification ticket sent by the show superintendent, noting the time you must be there and place where the show will be held, as well as time of judging.

If you have kept your dog's coat in good condition by weekly grooming, there is little to do the day before the show. Groom him thoroughly from the skin out again, and be particularly careful to work out mats, to clean the dog's teeth and if necessary wash his feet and legs if the dirt cannot be brushed out.

Entries close about three weeks in advance for the larger or "point" shows. You will probably want to enter your dog in novice, or in puppy class if he is between six and twelve months of age.

Don't feed your dog the morning of the show, or give him at most a light meal. He will be more comfortable in the car on the way, and will show more enthusiastically. When you arrive at the show grounds, you should find his assigned bench and settle him there.

Take your dog to the exercise ring to relieve himself, and give him a final grooming, then wait at the ring for your class to be called. All male classes are first, in this order: Puppy, Novice, Bred by Exhibitor, American bred, Open.

The winners in each class compete for Winners Dog. The Winners Dog is awarded points toward his championship according to the number of dogs present in the classes within the particular breed. The same procedure is followed in bitches; these first place winners in each class compete for Winners Bitch. Also designated by the judge are the Reserve Winners Dog and the Reserve Winners Bitch. However, only the Winners Dog and Winners Bitch, not the Reserve winners receive points. The dog and bitch then compete against each other for Best of Winners, and they also vie with the champions in the Specials class for Best of Breed and for Best of Opposite Sex to Best of Breed.

Best of Breed is the highest-placing dog in a given breed, and that winner then represents the particular breed in Group competition. Groups include: Sporting Dogs, Hounds, Working Dogs, Terriers, Toys, and Non-sporting Dogs. The judge of each Group selects first, second, third, and fourth place among the Best of Breed winners within specific Groups. First-place winners in each Group then compete for Best in Show.

A scale of points is printed in each dog show catalog, and the number of points awarded in a breed depends on the number of dogs shown in competition. A win of three or more points at a show is called a "major." To attain championship, a dog must win a total of fifteen points under at least three different judges, and included in those fifteen points must be two majors (each under a different judge). A dog that accumulates fifteen points and no majors does not qualify for championship. A dog must win in keen competition.

Other aspects of dog shows are the obedience trials and the field trials. Any purebred dog may compete, and each is judged on performance rather than conformation. Many dogs that have already earned their championship in the conformation ring also compete for obedience and field trial degrees.

There are three classes in obediences: novice, open, and utility. Tracking tests also are held. The respective degrees earned are: C.D., C.D.X., U.D., and T.D. These are: Companion Dog, Companion Dog Excellent, Utility Dog, and Tracking Dog. To earn a C.D., both the dog and his handler must perform six exercises together to the satisfaction of three different judges. Judges score the teams on a scale of zero to two hundred points, and a score of 170 points or higher earns a dog a "leg" toward his obedience degree. A dog must achieve three "legs" for a C.D. Exercises in this novice class are: heel on lead, stand for examination by a judge, heel off lead, do a long sit (sitting for a required number of minutes), do a long down (being down for several minutes), and recall (returning to his owner when called). After a dog gets his C.D., he then may try for his C.D.X. in Open obedience where he must jump over obstacles, retrieve items, and do more difficult exercises in three different trials. To achieve a U.D. title, a dog must do directed retrieving, jumping, and scent discrimination. To obtain a tracking degree, a dog competes in field trials where he "tracks" or follows a scent.

SOME CANINE SHOW TERMS

Understanding basic terminology in dogs is helpful. Terms such as "brisket," "stifle," "pastern," "hock," and so forth refer to specific parts of the anatomy of the dog, regardless of breed. In measuring the height of a dog, for example, you measure from the "withers" to the ground, the withers being the highest point of the shoulder and the place at which the back meets the base of the neck. You also hear the expression "good bone" in dogs. You can evaluate bone simply by grasping a front paw and feeling whether it is strong or slight. The latter is referred to as "fine in bone." "Weedy" is another expression regarding insufficient bone.

"Soundness" deals with the condition and structure of a dog. If sound, a dog is in good physical and mental condition. "Movement" is a way of evaluating soundness. If a dog moves properly (with a level back, head erect, forelegs reaching, and hindlegs driving), the animal demonstrates soundness. "Type" is another basic term in dogs. This concerns the specific characteristics that stamp a dog and indicate whether the animal is a hound, a terrier, a spaniel, etc. A dog is "typey" if specific breed characteristics are exemplified.

Dogs have "hackles," which is hair on the back of the neck. It is a sign of anger if a dog's hackles are raised. Dogs have upper and lower thighs in the hindlegs, and the "stifle" is the joint between the two thighs, somewhat like a knee; the "hock" is the ankle in each of the rear legs. The forelegs have elbows where they meet the "brisket" or the lower chest, and they have a wrist which is known as the "pastern" above the paws. If a dog is "down in pastern," the forelegs are not straight.

The "muzzle" of course is the foreface from the eyes to the nose. The "stop" is between the eyes, and the "occiput" is the point of the skull between the ears. "Expression" is the total look of the face.

The figure on the left demonstrates a poor front on a dog and shows how the dog is "out at the elbows." The figure on the right indicates a poor rear on a dog and shows how the dog is "cowhocked."

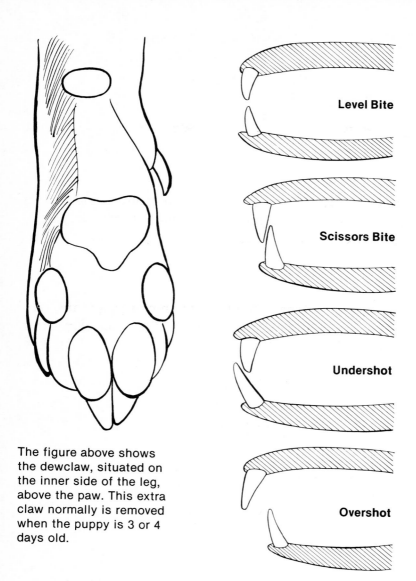

Level Bite

Scissors Bite

Undershot

Overshot

The figure above shows the dewclaw, situated on the inner side of the leg, above the paw. This extra claw normally is removed when the puppy is 3 or 4 days old.

The figures show four types of bites. At the top is a level bite, in which the upper and lower front teeth meet edge to edge. Next is the scissors bite—the inside of the upper teeth touch the outside of the lower teeth in the front of the mouth. When the lower front teeth project beyond those of the upper teeth, the jaw is undershot. When the upper front teeth project beyond the lower front teeth, the jaw is overshot.

Recommended Reading

THE ORIGINAL COMPLETE DOG BOOK by Dr. William Bruette and Kerry V. Donnelly, 608 pp., revised 1982, published by T.F.H. Publications, Inc., Neptune, New Jersey. This book is Kerry V. Donnelly's updated version of William A. Bruette's classic, first published under the title THE COMPLETE DOG BOOK in 1921, and should not be confused with any official publication of the American Kennel Club. This is the *only* book which contains complete standards for all breeds and which is kept up to date on an annual basis.

HUTCHINSON'S POPULAR & ILLUSTRATED DOG ENCYCLOPAEDIA by Walter Hutchinson, 3 volumes, alphabetically arranged for easy reference on breeds of dogs from every country. This collector's item is currently out of print but was published in 1949 and printed in Great Britain at The Anchor Press, Tiptree, Essex. The commentary, the pictures, and the drawings provide fascinating material and vividly portray the wonderful world of dogs.

DOGS AND PUPPIES edited by Douglas James with contributions from Wendy Boorer, Judy deCasembroot, Alan Hitchins, John Holmes, Mary Holmes, Howard Loxton, Margaret Osborne, Mary Roslin-Williams, and Barbara Woodhouse, 160 pp., published by Longmeadow Press, Norwalk, Connecticut, 1977. In this book, various breeds are pictured in their respective functions for which they were bred. Emphasis is on the care, training, and health of the dog.

THE WORLD OF DOGS by Wendy Boorer, 141 pp., published by The Hamlyn Publishing Group Limited, London, New York, Sydney, Toronto, 1969, has a lively text and lovely pictures about all aspects of the dog.

THE LIFE, HISTORY AND MAGIC OF THE DOG by Fernand Mery, 235 pp., published by Grosset & Dunlap, Inc., New York, as an English translation in 1970. Here is a book that ponders why the dog is cherished as a domesticated animal and delves deeper than superficial sentimentalism. The dog is depicted in history, literature, art, law, medicine, psychology, etc.

SUCCESSFUL DOG SHOW EXHIBITING by Anna Katherine Nicholas, 256 pp., published by T.F.H. Publications, Inc., Neptune, New Jersey. This is the ultimate how-to manual for purebred dog owners who contemplate entering the challenging world of show dog competition. It is a valuable reference book for novice through experienced show competitor by a judge who's been in the business for fifty years.

THE RIGHT DOG FOR YOU by Daniel F. Tortora, Ph.D., 381 pp., published by Simon & Schuster, New York, 1980. This book presents a systematic way of choosing a breed that matches your personality, family, and lifestyle.

DOG OWNERS' VETERINARY GUIDE by G.W. Stamm, 112 pp., published by T.F.H. Publications, Inc., Neptune, New Jersey. This accurate book, based on information set forth by foremost veterinarians, is for the dog owner who is not familiar with the elements of diagnosis and treatment as well as for the owner who has some knowledge of medical practice.

ILLUSTRATED TEXTBOOK OF DOG DISEASES by The TV Vet, 192 pp., published by T.F.H. Publications, Inc., Neptune, New Jersey. This book provides a thorough-going knowledge of the cause, symptoms, and treatment for almost every illness or adverse health condition the dog owner will ever have occasion to deal with, whether your pet is pedigreed or of mixed parentage.

DOG OWNER'S ENCYCLOPEDIA OF VETERINARY MEDICINE by Allan H. Hart, B.V.Sc., published by T.F.H. Publications, Inc., Neptune, New Jersey. Written by a veterinarian who feels that most dog owners should recognize the symptoms and understand the cures of most diseases of dogs so they can properly communicate with their veterinarian, this book is a necessity for every dog owner.

DOGS AND HOW TO BREED THEM by Hilary Harmar, 299 pp., published by T.F.H. Publications, Inc., Neptune, New Jersey. Easily understood by the beginner, this book clearly introduces some of the many pitfalls in breeding. It gives in detail the procedures in mating and whelping for dogs of all sizes and follows up with some of the difficulties and complications which may occur.

DOG GENETICS by Dr. Carmen L. Battaglia, 192 pp., published by T.F.H. Publications, Inc., Neptune, New Jersey. This book is for the amateur breeder who would like to easily understand genetics. It focuses on the basics, simplifies the heavy technical jargon, puts forth an easy-to-understand plan for breeding, and clarifies many of the misconceptions surrounding the subject.

DOG BREEDING FOR PROFESSIONALS by Dr. Herbert Richards, 224 pp., published by T.F.H. Publications, Inc., Neptune, New Jersey. This book is for dog owners who need and actively seek good advice about how to go about breeding their dogs.

DOG BREEDING by Ernest H. Hart, 223 pp., published by T.F.H. Publications, Inc., Neptune, New Jersey. This book covers the physiology of the bitch and stud dog, gestation, whelping, fertility, how to build a strain, and environment and heredity.

DOG BEHAVIOR by Ian Dunbar, published by T.F.H. Publications, Inc., Neptune, New Jersey. This book is for everyone who likes dogs and wants to understand them better as well as for anyone interested in animal behavior. Written in a charming and witty style, it is both informative and entertaining.

GOOD FOOD FOR YOUR DOG by Jean Powell, 77 pp., published by Citadel Press, Secaucus, New Jersey, 1980. The importance of proper diet and nutrition is set forward in an organized and interesting manner.

DOG TRAINING by Lew Burke, 255 pp., published by T.F.H. Publications, Inc., Neptune, New Jersey. In this book, the elements of dog training are easy to grasp and apply. The author uses dogs' psychological makeup to his advantage by making them want to be what they should be, substituting the family for the pack.

HOW TO TRAIN YOUR DOG by Ernest H. Hart, 107 pp., published by T.F.H. Publications, Inc., Neptune, New Jersey. This is a must for owner and dog. The author teaches the quickest and easiest route to canine training.